Rocket Reader 1

By

Carol Anne Campodonica

Copyright 2024, 2023

Public School, Charter School, Home School, and Libraries.

Struggling middle school, junior high and high school students coaching lessons at home.

School Libraries and County Libraries may purchase a copy of Rocket Reader 1 for parents to use at home. Each young person needs the opportunity to read successfully.

No copies can be made, physical or digital, without the consent of the author.

Introduction

Rocket Reader 1 was created for parents, new teachers, experienced teachers, or substitutes. Reading is complex. And every student can benefit from practicing the necessary skills. Words have been provided for the adult to identify the sounds that make up a word.

Consonants, vowels, blends, digraphs, and diphthongs can be heard in reading the sight words. Consonants, blends, digraphs never change their sounds. Only vowels change their sounds. It should be taught in the above order. Primary learns long and short vowel sounds.

Young children should know the difference between an upper-and-lower case letters of the alphabet. Confidence begins when a child can read a letter, know the sound of the letter, and can read a word.

Older children can master three words that have the same vowel sound. Each word is to be written on a separate index card. A quick response is reading builds confidence and a desire to learn. Introduce one set at a time and practice.

Sight words are shown, and they are not in alphabetical order. Students may memorize the order of words instead of reading the words. Place words on index cards with a large Sharpie marker. Shuffle the deck and review the words learned and those that are sight words. Two quick snaps of the finger is the response time for reading a word on an index card.

<u>Exaggerate the Vowel Sounds</u>

Visually a student can see a vowel within a word (a, e, i, o, u). The sound of a long "a" and a short "a" may not be heard. Students need to hear the difference between a long "a" sound and a short "a" sound. All students should imitate the exaggerated vowel sound to hear the difference between a long "a" and a short "a" sounds, examples of this can be found on page four.

With ***two vowels*** together the ***first vowel*** letter is **heard,** and the second letter is silent. Never introduce a new word until the student hears the difference and can imitate the word with a long and short exaggerated vowel sound.

An "e" at the end of a sight word is silent and makes the vowel long. We call it saying its name rule. All vowels in a word with an "e" at the end of the word will make a vowel long.

In the list of sight words, students will hear and see the blends, digraphs, and diphthongs. Instructors should place words on index cards for students. The adult may ask questions using decoding pattern that is given on each page of Rocket Reader 1. State tests will have students identify consonants, vowels, blends, digraphs, and diphthongs within a word.

Memorization concerning the order of letters is important for reading and spelling words. Some people may not be capable of hearing a particular sound and will need to memorize the word.

A pronunciation key provides words rather than accent marks.

There are several different ways of asking for the sounds of letters. For primary and younger students, the adult should use the number 1 example listed below.

Older students can be given two different questions to identify the sound of a letter. (The three ways numbered are good). Number one is the best for kindergarten-first grade students.

1. "k" sounds like?

2. The "k" sounds like?

3. What sound does a "k" make?

Use a lot of positive comments while teaching or coaching your child. Such as: great, wonderful, excellent, super, fabulous, marvelous, superior, superb, splendid, remarkable, cool, spectacular, amazing, and impressive. These will help build the confidence of a child learning math.

Pronunciation

To help pronounce a word, bold faced letters are used to indicate the sound within key word.

s**a**t = short (a) sound.
ate = long (a) sound.
about = schwa sound of (uh).
c**a**re = (air) sound.
p**aw** = (aw) sound.

b**e**t = short (e) sound.
b**ee**t = long (e) sound. (In alike vowels, first vowel is heard).
h**er** = (er).

s**i**t = short (i) sound.
ice = long (i) sound.

dr**o**p = short (o) sound.
b**o**at = long (o) sound.
din**o**saur = schwa sound (uh)

bo**o**k = (took) closed sound.
m**oo**n = (snooze) open sound.
bo**u**ght = (aw) sound.

b**u**t = short (u) sound.
use = long (u) sound

Consonants

An immediate response on knowing the sound of a letter is one snap of a finger for older students who are struggling in reading at school.

Toddlers or first graders must see each one of the letters on an index card. Toddlers must recognize the letter and the sound. Periodically throughout the day, show the index card and ask the child to produce the sound of the letter (five times). Remember toddlers do not sit for long periods of time. They need to recognize upper-and-lower case letters.

B, C, D, F, G, H, J, K, L, M, N, P, Q, R, S, T, V, W, X, Y, Z

b = bat	c = cat	d = dog	f = fat	g = goat	h = hat
j = jacket	k = key	l = locket	m = mop	n = nap	p = pill
q = quick	r = red	s = salad	t = top	v = voice	w = wax
x = x-ray	y = yellow	z = zebra			

Blends

Blends must be memorized according to the order of letters for state testing and to identify a blend in a word. In a blend, both letters will be heard. Place letters on index cards, shuffle the deck and have the young person respond quickly. A slow response requires more practice to become a smooth reader of words.

bl = blue	fr = freeze	pr = prince	sp = space	br = broom
gr = grow	sc = scout	st = statue	cl = clown	gl = glow
sk = skip	sw = swim	dr = drum	gr = grow	sl = slip
tr = train	fl = flower	pl = plate	sn = snake	tw = twin

Digraphs

Two consonant letters make up a digraph. Each digraph has one sound that is heard. Recognizing digraph sounds will help students to read a sentence fluently. Place each digraph on an index card and practice the one sound it makes.

gh = ghost	sh = cash	th = father	ck = check
ph = phone (f).	wr = write	wh = white	ch = church
kn = knife	ss = chess	tch = watch	

"Ch" has three sounds.
1. church = (ch).
2. chef = (sh).
3. school = (k).

Diphthongs

Diphthongs have two vowels while other diphthongs have a vowel and a consonant. Some diphthongs may have more than one sound. On one index card write the word and the sound on one side and just the word on the opposite side.

1. Ow or ou
Ow=clown
Ou=pout

2. I, Y, igh, Ie
I=my
Y=sky
Igh=light
Ie=tied

3. Oy or oi
Oy=oyster
Oi=boil

4. Ow or Oa
Ow=snow
Oa=toad

5. Ai or Ay
Ai=faith
Ay=bay

6. U, Ue, Eu, Ew
U=Tune
Ue=due
Eu=Europe
Ew=few

7. Ea or E
Ea=see
Ea=sea
E=pier

8. Ai, A, Ea
Ai=rain
A=able
Ea=break

Triple Consonants

One additional consonant letter added to a blend or digraph makes a triple consonant. *Most being with an "s".*

nth = ninth	spr = spring	sch = school	squ = squash
shr = shrill	str = string	spl = splash	thr = three

Apple

Words are complex because irregularity may occur in a word. For example, "apple" does not have a long "**a**" but has a ***short*** "a" sound. An "**e**" is at the **end** of the word and it usually makes a vowel **long**.

Sight words have been provided but not all of them. Primary children must hear the difference between a long and short "a" vowel sound. Exaggeration is important for the listener to hear. It will help by reading the sentence provided with a long "a" and a short "a" vowel sound. They will listen to the sentence and decide which vowel sound is correct when pronouncing the word.

Older students will need to know and hear the difference in vowel sounds other than long and the short vowel sounds. The "a" has different sounds, but only five have been provided in the pronunciation key. Students need to be capable of reading a sight word without hesitating.

Long Vowel Words: gate, rate, bait

1. Long: g-a-a-a-a-a-t = gate.   The gate was closed. ***Repeat the sentence by stretching out the long "a" sound and then repeat the word with a short "a" sound.***

2. Long: r-a-a-a-a-a-a-t-e = rate.   How would you rate my paper?

3. Long: b-a-a-a-a-a-a-i-t = bait.   I will get the fish bait.

Short Vowel Words: fat, rat, mat

1. Short: f-a-a-a-a-a-a-t = fat. My cat is too fat. *Repeat sentence with a short "a" sound and then a long "a" sound (fate). Exaggerate and have students exaggerate the short and long "a" sound.*

2. Short: r-a-a-a-a-a-a-t = rat. We trapped the rat. (rate)

3. Short: m-a-a-a-a-a-a-t = mat. He sat on the mat. (mate)

In teaching reading, readers will learn the long and short sound of the following vowels of (a, e, i, o, u) before learning additional vowel sounds.

Students in middle, junior high or high school are encouraged to master the additional vowel sounds.

Schwa sound: Schwa has an "uh" sound. A grunting sound.

EXAMPLES

1. I hate to get **up** early. *Say the word up. Up has a "uh" sound.*
2. My **uncle** hates to clean the toilet. Say the word **uncle** = "uh" sound.
3. It is **about** time to get up.
4. I'm **afraid** of the dark.
5. The s**a**lad needs a tomato.
6. Do you want to get a s**u**b sandwich for lunch?
7. **Aug**ust is a wonderful month.
8. My sk**u**ll hurts.
9. Th**e** boys went swimming.

A hard "r" sound is heard when "ar" is present. Examples:

1. The ice cream **bar** is closed.
2. How **far** is the Lake Mead.

Some vowels with an "a" in the word have an "ah" sound.

Examples:

1. My **f<u>a</u>ther** is tall (ah).
2. I am an **<u>au</u>thor** of books (ah).
3. The **p<u>a</u>dre** was late for work (ah).

A pattern for decoding a one syllable word has been provided.

The consonant "e" in a ***one*** syllable word. It is silent when it is written at the end of a word. Spell the word. Students will read the word aloud. Example: Say each letter **"r-a-t-<u>e</u>."**

1. The "e" sounds like? (silent)
2. The "t" sounds like?
3. The "a" sounds like? Is the "a" long or short? (**long**)
4. The "r" sounds like?
5. "r-a-t-e" sounds like?
6. Quickly read the word aloud.

Example: Say each letter **"b-<u>a</u>-i-t."** **Rule:** *Two vowels together make the second vowel silent and the first vowel long.*

b**<u>a</u>i**t:
1. The "t" sounds like?
2. The "i" sounds like?
3. The "a" sounds like?
4. The "b" sounds like?
5. "b-a-i-t" sounds like?
6. Quickly read the word aloud.

Decoding Blends

blends:
1. The "s" sounds like?
2. The "d" sounds like?
3. The "n" sounds like?
4. The "e" sounds like?
5. The "l" sounds like?

                6. The "b" sounds like?
                7. "b-l-e-n-d-s" sounds like?
                8. Quickly read the word aloud.

blank: 1. The "k" sounds like?
                2. The "n" sounds like?
                3. The "a" sounds like?
                4. The "l" sounds like?
                5. The "b" sounds like?
                6. "b-l-a-n-k" sounds like?
                7. Quickly read the word aloud.

blink: 1. The "k" sounds like?
                2. The "n" sounds like?
                3. The "i" sounds like?
                4. The "l sounds like?
                5. The "b" sounds like?
                6. "b-l-i-n-k" sounds like.
                7. Quickly read the word aloud.

E Vowel

Long "e" words: see, me,

1. s-e-e-e-e-e-e-e = see. <u>Can you **see** the picture?</u>
   What are the two vowels?
   Which vowel is silent?
   Which vowel is long?

2. m-e-e-e-e-e-e = me. <u>Will you sit with **me**</u>?
   Which vowel is silent?
   Which vowel is longer?

Short "e" vowels: met, get.

    1. m-e-e-e-e-e-e-t = met. <u>I **met** you last week.</u>

    2. g-e-e-e-e-e-e-t = get. <u>Will you **get** the mail?</u>

<h3 style="text-align:center"><u>I Vowel</u></h3>

Long "i" vowel: pie, mice, rice

    1. p-i-i-i-i-i-i-e = pie. <u>The **pie** was good.</u>

    2. m-i-i-i-i-i-i-c-e = mice. <u>We have no **mice** in the house.</u>

    3. r-i-i-i-i-i-i-c-e = rice. <u>Let us eat **rice** for dinner.</u>

Short "i" sound: rich, sift, cliff.

r<u>i</u>ch:
    1. "c-h" sounds like?
    2. "i" sounds like?
    3. "r" sounds like?
    4. "r-i-c-h" sounds like?
    5. Quickly read the word aloud.

s<u>i</u>ft:
    1. "t" sounds like?
    2. "f" sounds like?
    3. "i" sounds like?
    4. "s" sounds like?
    5. "s-i-f-t" sounds like?
    6. Quickly read the word aloud.

cl<u>i</u>ff:
    1. "f-f" sounds like?
    2. "i" sound like?
    3. "l" sound like?
    4. "c" sound like?

5. "c-l-i-f-f" sounds like?
6. Quickly read the word aloud.

O Vowel

Long "o" Vowels: open, over, okay

    1. o-o-o-o-p-e-n = open. <u>Do not **open** the door.</u>

    2. o-o-o-o-v-e-r = over. <u>We will jump **over** the fence.</u>

    3. o-o-o-o-k-a-y = okay. <u>**Okay,** I will make a cake.</u>

Short "o" Vowels: pop, mop, hop.

    1. p-o-o-o-o-p = pop. <u>Do not **pop** the balloons.</u>

    2. m-o-o-o-o-n = moon. <u>I will **mop** the floor.</u>

    3. h-o-o-o-o-p = hop. <u>Did you see Ted **hop**?</u>

Two "o" vowels may be **closed** or **open** in sound. *Exaggerate for students to hear. Student should imitate the sound.*

closed sound.   1. b-o-o-o-o-o-o-k = book. <u>The **book** is on the desk.</u>

                    2. c-o-o-o-o-o-o-k = cook. <u>Mary will **cook**.</u>

                      3. t-o-o-o-o-o-o-k = took. <u>Jane **took** my cup.</u>

open sound.   1. c-o-o-o-o-o-o-l = cool. <u>Bill has a **cool** car.</u>

                      2. m-o-o-o-o-o-n = moon. <u>The **moon** is full tonight.</u>

3. s-o-o-o-o-o-n = soon.   Summer will be here **soon.**

Oi Vowels

"oi" vowel words: noise, voice, join, oil.

1. n- oi-oi-oi-oi-oi-se = noise. Airplanes make a lot of **noise.**

2. v- oi-oi-oi-oi-oi-ce = voice. Have you lost your **voice**?

3. j-oi-oi-oi-oi-oi-n = join. I will **join** the family soon.

4. oi-oi-oi-oi-oi-oi-l = oil. Olive **oil** tastes good on a salad.

"ou" vowel words: out, cloud, foul, about. ("ou are vowels as well as diphthongs).

1. ou-ou-ou-ou-ou-t = out. My aunt is **out** to lunch.

2. c-l- ou-ou-ou-ou-d = cloud. The **cloud** is dark.

3. f-ou-ou-ou-ou-ou-l = foul. He hit a **foul** ball.

4. a-b-ou-ou-ou-ou-t = about. I am **about** to quit selling cars.

Long U Vowel

Long "u" words: music, pupil, uniform, unit.

1. m-u-u-u-u-u-s-ic = music. I play the piano **music.**

2. p-u-u-u-u-u-p-i-l = pupil. Joe is a **pupil** in first grade.

3. u-u-u-u-u-u-u-n-i-f-o-r-m = uniform. My band **uniform** is red.

4. u-u-u-u-u-u-n-i-t = unit. <u>Tim is reading **unit** one.</u>

Short "u" words: bug, rug, pup, cup.

1. b-u-u-u-u-u-g = bug. <u>The **bug** is on the cake.</u>

2. r-u-u-u-u-u-u-g = rug. <u>We must clean the **rug.**</u>

3. p-u-u-u-u-u-u-p = pup. <u>Where did the **pup** go?</u>

4. c-u-u-u-u-u-u-p = cup. <u>Where is my **cup** of coffee?</u>

Schwa "u" words: ugly, uncle, under, umbrella

1. u-u-u-u-u-u-u-g-l-y= ugly. <u>The **ugly** duckling is swimming.</u>

2. u-u-u-u-u-u-u-n-c-l-e = uncle. <u>My **uncle** Sam is here.</u>

3. u-u-u-u-u-u-u-n-d-er = under. <u>We are sitting **under** the oak tree.</u>

4. u-u-u-u-u-m-br-e-ll-a = umbrella. <u>We left the **umbrella** at home.</u>

Long "a" vowel: ate, make, fake.

<u>a</u>te:
1. "e" sounds like? (silent).
2. "t" sounds like?
3. "a" sounds like?
4. "a-t-e" sounds like?
5. Quickly read the word aloud.

m<u>a</u>ke:
1. "e" sounds like? (silent).
2. "k" sounds like?
3. "a" sounds like?

4. "m" sounds like?
5. "m-a-k-e" sounds like? Read it quickly.

f<u>a</u>ke:
1. "e" sounds like?
2. "k" sounds like?
3. "a" sounds like?
4. "f" sounds like?
5. "f-a-k-e" sounds like?
6. Quickly read the word aloud.

Short "a" vowel: cat, can, man

c<u>a</u>t:
1. "t" sounds like?
2. "a" sounds like?
3. "c" sounds like?
4. "c-a-t" sounds like?
5. Quickly read the word aloud.

c<u>a</u>n:
1. "n" sounds like?
2. "a" sounds like?
3. "c" sounds like?
4. "c-a-n" sounds like?
5. Quickly read the word aloud.

m<u>a</u>n:
1. "n" sounds like?
2. "a" sounds like?
3. "m" sounds like?
4. "m-a-n" sounds like?
5. Quickly read the word aloud.

Long "e" vowel: beet, seat, deep

b<u>ee</u>t:
1. "t" sounds like?
2. "e-e" sounds like?

      3. "b" sounds like?
      4. "b-e-e-t" sounds like?
      5. Quickly read the word aloud.

s<u>ea</u>t: 1. "t" sounds like?
      2. "a" sounds like?
      3. "e" sounds like?
      4. "s" sounds like?
      5. "s-e-a-t" sounds like?
      6. Quickly read the word aloud.

d<u>ee</u>p: 1. "p" sounds like?
      2. "e-e" sounds like?
      3. "d" sounds like?
      4. "d-e-e-p" sounds like?
      5. Quickly read the word aloud.

Long "i" vowel sound: ice, nice, pie

<u>i</u>ce: 1. "e" sounds like?
      2. "c" sounds like? (s).
      3. "i" sounds like?
      4. "i-c-e" sounds like?
      5. Quickly read the word aloud.

n<u>i</u>ce: 1. "e" sounds like?
      2. "c" sounds like?
      3. "i" sounds like?
      4. "n" sounds like?
      5. "n-i-c-e "sounds like?
      6. Quickly read the word aloud.

Short "i" vowels: pit, tip, sip.

p<u>i</u>t:
1. "t" sounds like?
2. "i" sounds like?
3. "p" sounds like?
4. "p-i-t" sounds like?
5. Quickly read the word aloud.

t<u>i</u>p:
1. "p" sounds like?
2. "i" sounds like?
3. "t" sounds like?
4. "t-i-p" sounds like?
5. Quickly read the word aloud.

s<u>i</u>p:
1. "p" sounds like?
2. "i" sounds like?
3. "s" sounds like?
4. "s-i-p" sounds like?
5. Quickly read the word aloud.

Long "o" vowels: open, poke, go

<u>o</u>pen:
1. "n" sounds like?
2. "e" sounds like?
3. "p" sounds like?
4. "o" sounds like?
5. "o-p-e-n" sounds like?
6. Quickly read the word aloud.

p<u>o</u>ke:
1. "e" sounds like?
2. "k" sounds like?
3. "o" sounds like?
4. "p" sounds like?
5. "p-o-k-e" sounds like?
6. Quickly read the word aloud.

g**o**: 1. "o" sounds like?
      2. "g" sounds like?
      3. "g-o" sounds like?
      4. Quickly read the word aloud.

Short "o" vowels: top, stop, crop.

t**o**p: 1. "p" sounds like?
      2. "o" sounds like?
      3. "t" sounds like?
      4. "t-o-p" sounds like?
      5. Quickly read the word aloud.

st**o**p: 1. "p" sounds like?
      2. "o" sounds like?
      3. "t" sounds like?
      4. "s" sounds like?
      5. "s-t-o-p" sounds like?
      6. Quickly read the word aloud.

cr**o**p: 1. "p" sounds like?
      2. "o" sounds like?
      3. "r" sounds like?
      4. "c" sounds like?
      5. "c-r-o-p" sounds like?
      6. Quickly read the word aloud.

Long "u" vowel: use, cube, music

use: 1. "e" sounds like? (silent).
      2. "s" sounds like?
      3. "u" sounds like?
      4. "u-s-e" sounds like?

5. Quickly read the word aloud.

c<u>u</u>be:
1. "e" sounds like?
2. "b" sounds like?
3. "u" sounds like?
4. "c" sounds like?
5. c-u-b-e sounds like? Quickly read the word aloud.

m<u>u</u>sic:
1. "c" sounds like?
2. "i" sounds like?
3. "s" sounds like?
4. "u" sounds like?
5. "m" sounds like?
6. "m-u-s-i-c" sounds like?
7. Quickly read the word aloud.

Short "u" vowel: bun, must, sun.

b<u>u</u>n:
1. "n" sounds like?
2. "u" sounds like?
3. "b" sounds like?
4. "b-u-n" sounds like?
5. Quickly read the word aloud.

m<u>u</u>st:
1. "t" sounds like?
2. "s" sounds like?
3. "u" sounds like?
4. "m" sounds like?
5. "m-u-s-t" sounds like?
6. Quickly read the word aloud.

s<u>u</u>n:
1. "n" sounds like?
2. "u" sounds like?
3. "s" sounds like?
4. "s-u-n" sounds like?
5. Quickly read the word aloud.

Open sound with two **"oo" words**. **"oo"** words = soon, moon, food. *Student may place index finger on their throat to feel the **open** and **closed** sound of the double "oo" vowel letters.*

s<u>oo</u>n:
    1. "n" sounds like?
    2. "o-o" sounds like?
    3. "s" sounds like?
    4. "s-o-o-n" sounds like?
    5. Read word quickly.

m<u>oo</u>n:
    1. "n" sounds like?
    2. "o-o" sounds like?
    3. "m" sounds like?
    4. "m-o-o-n" sounds like?
    5. Quickly read the word aloud.

f<u>oo</u>d:
    1. "d" sounds like?
    2. "o-o" sounds like?
    3. "f" sounds like?
    4. "f-o-o-d" sounds like?
    5. Quickly read the word aloud.

"ui" = "oo" (open sound): fruit, juice, cruise.

fr<u>ui</u>t:
    1. "t" sounds like?
    2. "u-i" sounds like?
    3. "r" sounds like?
    4. "f" sounds like?
    5. "f-r-u-i-t" sounds like?
    6. Quickly read the word.

j<u>ui</u>ce:
    1. "e" sounds like?
    2. "c" sounds like?
    3. "u-i" sounds like?
    4. "j" sounds like?

                    5. "j-u-i-c-e" sounds like?
                    6. Quickly read the word aloud.

cr**ui**se: 1. "e" sounds like?
               2. "s" sounds like?
               3. "u-i" sounds like?
               4. "r" sounds like?
               5. "c" sounds like?
               6. "c-r-u-i-s-e" sounds like?
               7 Quickly read the word aloud.

"ee" words = long "e": sheet, peep, seed.

sh**ee**t: 1. "t" sounds like?
               2. "e-e" sounds like?
               3. "s-h" sounds like?
               4. "s-h-e-e-t" sounds like?
               5. Quickly read the word aloud.

p**ee**p: 1. The last "p" sounds like?
               2. "e-e" sounds like?
               3. The first "p" sounds like?
               4. "p-e-e-p" sounds like?
               5. Quickly read the word aloud.

s**ee**d: 1. "d" sounds like?
               2. "e-e" sounds like?
               3. "s" sounds like?
               4. "s-e-e-d" sounds like?
               5. Quickly read the word aloud.

"ar" words = hard "r": car, dart, start

c**ar**:   1. "a-r" sounds like?
               2. "c" sounds like?
               3. "c-a-r" sounds like?
               4. Quickly read the word aloud.

d**ar**t: 1. "t" sounds like?
               2. "a-r" sounds like?
               3. "d" sounds like?
               4. "d-a-r-t" sounds like?
               5. Quickly read the word aloud?

st**ar**t: 1. "t" sounds like?
               2. "a-r" sounds like?
               3. "t" sounds like?
               4. "s" sounds like?
               5. "s-t-a-r-t" sounds like?
               6. Quickly read the word aloud.

"ar" = air sound: marry, bare, care

m**ar**ry: 1. "y" sounds like?
               2. "r" sounds like?
               3. "a-r" sounds like?
               4. "m" sounds like?
               5. "m-a-r-r-y" sounds like?
               6. Quickly read the word aloud.

b**are**:   1. "e" sounds like?
               2. "a-r" sounds like?
               3. "b" sounds like?
               4. "b-a-r-e" sounds like?
               5. Quickly read the word aloud.

c<u>ar</u>e:	1. "e" sounds like?
2. "a-r" sounds like?
3. "c" sounds like?
4. "c-a-r-e" sounds like?
5. Quickly read the word aloud.

"ay" words = long "a": day, bay, say

d**ay**:	1. "y" sounds like? (silent)
2. "a" sounds like?
3. "d" sounds like?
4. "d-a-y sounds like?
5. Quickly read the word aloud.

b**ay**:	1. "y" sounds like?
2. "a" sounds like?
3. "b" sounds like?
4. "b-a-y" sounds like?
5. Quickly read the word aloud.

s**ay**:	1. "y" sounds like?
2. "a" sounds like?
3. "s" sounds like?
4. "s-a-y" sounds like?
5. Quickly read the word aloud.

"y" words = long "i": sly, fly, shy

sl**y**:	1. "y" sounds like?
2. "l" sounds like?
3. "s" sounds like?
4. "s-l-y" sounds like?
5. Quickly read the word aloud.

fl**y**: 1. "y" sounds like?
2. "l" sounds like?
3. "f" sounds like?
4. "f-l-y" sounds like?
5. Quickly read the word aloud.

sh**y**: 1. "y" sounds like?
2. "s-h" sounds like?
3. "s-h-y" sounds like?
4. Quickly read the word aloud.

"y" = long "e": carry, berry, happy

carr**y**: 1. "y" sounds like?
2. "r" sounds like?
3. "a-r" sounds like?
4. "c" sounds like?
5. "c-a-r-r-y" sounds like?
6. Quickly read the word aloud.

berr**y**: 1. "y" sounds like?
2. "r" sounds like?
3. "e-r" sounds like?
4. "b" sounds like?
5. "b-e-r-r-y" sounds like?
6. Quickly read the word aloud.

happ**y**: 1. "y" sounds like?
2. "p-p" sounds like?
3. "a" sounds like?
4. "h" sounds like?
5. "h-a-p-p-y" sounds like?
6. Quickly read the word aloud.

"ow" = long "o" sound: row, blow, snow.

r**ow**:
1. "o-w" sounds like?
2. "r" sounds like?
3. "r-o-w" sounds like?
4. Quickly read the word aloud.

bl**ow**:
1. "o-w" sounds like?
2. "l" sounds like?
3. "b" sounds like?
4. "b-l-o-w "sounds like?
5. Quickly read the word aloud.

sn**ow**:
1. "o-w" sounds like?
2. "n" sounds like?
3. "s" sounds like?
4. "s-n-o-w" sounds like?
5. Quickly read the word aloud.

Digraph "ow": cow, plow, sow

c**ow**:
1. "o-w" sounds like?
2. "c" sounds like?
3. "c-o-w" sounds like?
4. Quickly read the word aloud.

pl**ow**:
1. "o-w" sounds like?
2. "l" sounds like?
3. "p" sounds like?
4. "p-l-o-w" sounds like?
5. Quickly read the word aloud.

s**ow**: 1. "o-w" sounds like?
2. "s" sounds like?
3. "s-o-w" sounds like?
4. Quickly read the word aloud.

"er" words: her, after, clerk.

h**er**: 1. "e-r" sounds like?
2. "h" sounds like?
3. "h-e-r" sounds like?
4. Quickly read the word aloud.

aft**er**: 1. "e-r" sounds like?
2. "t" sounds like?
3. "f" sounds like?
4. "a" sounds like?
5. "a-f-t-e-r" sounds like?
6. Quickly read the word aloud.

cl**er**k 1. "k" sounds like?
2. "e-r" sounds like?
3. "l" sounds like?
4. "c" sounds like?
5. "c-l-e-r-k" sounds like?
6. Read word quickly.

"ea" words = long "e" sound: tea, eat, fleas

t**ea**: 1. "a" sounds like?
2. "e" sounds like?
3. "t" sounds like?
4. "t-e-a" sounds like?
5. Quickly read the word aloud.

eat: 1. "t" sounds like?
              2. "a" sounds like?
              3. "e" sounds like?
              4. "e-a-t" sounds like?
              5. Quickly read the word aloud.

fl**ea**s: 1. "s" sounds like?
              2. "a" sounds like?
              3. "e" sounds like?
              4. "l" sounds like?
              5. "f" sounds like?
              6. "f-l-e-a-s "sounds like?
              7. Quickly read the word aloud.

Digraph Words

Digraphs have two letters but make one sound. Digraphs can be found in the beginning, middle or end of a word which may be longer than a one syllable word. Some irregularities may be found in a standard rule regarding words.

Words that have a "**ph**" have an "**f**" sound: phone, graph, Philip.

phone: 1. "e" sounds like (silent).
              2. "n" sounds like?
              3. "o" sounds like?
              4. "p-h" sounds like?
              5. "p-h-o-n-e" sounds like?
              6. Quickly read the word aloud.

gra**ph:**   1. "p-h" sounds like?
              2. "a" sounds like?

                     3. "r" sounds like?
                     4. "g" sounds like?
                     5. "g-r-a-p-h" sounds like?
                     6. Quickly read the word aloud.

Philip: 1. "p" sounds like?
                     2. The second "i" sounds like?
                     3. "l" sounds like?
                     4. The first "i" sounds like?
                     5. "P-h" sounds like?
                     6. P-h-i-l-i-p sounds like?
                     7. Quickly read the word aloud.
                     8. Another name for "ph" is? **(Digraph)**

    Words with a "**gh**" at the end of a word have an "**f**" sound.
If the "gh" comes *after* an "**ou**" or "**au**" letter; the "gh" will have a "f" sound.
Some words may have a silent "gh" sound like in the word "bri**gh**t".

Digraphs "gh": tough, rough, laugh

        * These words include diphthongs "ow" and "ou" too *

t***ou*gh**:   1. "g-h" sounds like?
                     2. "o-u" sounds like?
                     3. "t" sounds like?
                     4. "t-o-u-g-h" sounds like?
                     5. Quickly read the word aloud.

r***ou*gh**:   1. "g-h" sounds like?
                     2. "o-u" sounds like?
                     3. "r" sounds like?
                     4. "r-o-u-g-h" sounds like?
                     5. Quickly read the word aloud.

l***au*gh**:   1. "g-h" sounds like?
                     2. "a-u" sounds like?

3. "l" sounds like?
4. "l-a-u-g-h" make?
5. Quickly read the word aloud.

Silent "gh": plough, dough, although.

pl*ough*:
1. "g-h" sounds like? (silent).
2. "o-u" sounds like? (ow sound)
3. "l" sounds like?
4. "p" sounds like?
5. "p-l-o-u-g-h" sounds like?
6. Quickly read the word aloud?

d*ough*:
1. "g-h" sounds like?
2. "o-u" sounds like?
3. "d" sounds like?
4. "d-o-u-g-h" sounds like?
5. Quickly read the word aloud.

alth*ough*:
1. "g-h" sounds like?
2. "o-u" sounds like?
3. "t-h" sounds like?
4. "l" sounds like?
5. "a" sounds like?
6. "a-l-t-h-o-u-g-h" sounds like?
7. Quickly read the word aloud.

*You do **not** hear the **gh** in the middle of the following words. (bright*, light, fight).

bri**gh**t:
1. "t" sounds like?
2. "g-h" sounds like? (silent).
3. "i" sounds like?
4. "r" sounds like?
5. "b" sounds like?

          6. "b-r-i-g-h-t" sounds like?
          7. Quickly read the word aloud.
          8. Another word for "b-r" is? **(blend)**

li**gh**t:
1. "t" sounds?
2. "g-h" sounds like?
3. "i" sounds like?
4. "l" sounds like?
5. "l-i-g-h-t" sounds like?
6. Quickly read the word aloud.

fi**gh**t:
1. "t" sounds like?
2. "g-h" sounds like?
3. "i" sounds like?
4. "f" sounds like?
5. "f-i-g-h-t" sounds like?
6. Quickly read the word aloud.

Digraph "ch": chill, attach, church.

chill:
1. "l-l" sounds like?
2. "i" sounds like?
3. "c-h" sounds like?
4. "c-h-i-l-l" sounds like?
5. Quickly read the word aloud.

atta**ch**:
1. "c-h" sounds like?
2. "a" sounds like?
3. "t-t" sounds like?
4. "a" sounds like?
5. "a-t-t-a-c-h" sounds like?
6. Quickly read the word aloud.

chur**ch**:   1. "c-h" sounds like?
                2. "r" sounds like?
                3. "u" sounds like?
                4. "c-h" sounds like?
                5. "c-h-u-r-c-h" sounds like?
                6. Quickly read the word aloud.

Digraph "th": these, them, the

these: 1. "e" sounds like?
                2. "s" sounds like?
                3. "e" sounds like?
                4. "t-h" sounds like?
                5. "t-h-e-s-e" sounds like?
                6. Quickly read the words aloud.

them: 1. "m" sounds like?
                2. "e" sounds like?
                3. "t-h" sounds like?
                4. "t-h-e-m" sounds like?
                5. Quickly read the word aloud.

the: 1. "e" sounds like?
                2. "t-h" sounds like?
                3. "t-h-e" sounds like?
                4. Quickly read the word aloud.

Digraph "wh": white, what, wharf.

white: 1. "e" sounds like?
                2. "t" sounds like?
                3. "i" sounds like?
                4. "w-h" sounds like?
                5. "w-h-i-t-e" sounds like?
                6. Quickly read the word aloud.

what: 1. "t" sounds like?
               2. "a" sounds like?
               3. "w-h" sounds like?
               4. "w-h-a-t" sounds like?
               5. Quickly read the word aloud.

wharf: 1. "f" sounds like?
               2. "r" sounds like?
               3. "a" sounds like?
               4. "w-h" sounds like"
               5. "w-h-a-r-f" sounds like?
               6. Quickly read the word aloud.

Combination "eigh" = long "a": eight, weight, sleigh

eight: 1. "t" sounds like?
               2. "e-i-g-h" sounds like?
               3. "e-i-g-h-t" sounds like?
               4. Quickly read the word aloud.

w**eigh**:   1. "e-i-g-h" sounds like?
               2. "w" sounds like?
               3. "w-e-i-g-h" sounds like?
               4. Quickly read the word aloud.

sl**eigh**:   1. "e-i-g-h" sounds like?
               2. "l" sounds like?
               3. "s" sounds like?
               4. "s-l-e-i-g-h "sounds like?
               5. Quickly say the word aloud.

Combination "ish": dish, wish, fish.

d<u>ish</u>:
1. "s-h" sounds like?
2. "i" sounds like?
3. "d" sounds like?
4. "d-i-s-h" sounds like?
5. Quickly read the word aloud

w<u>ish</u>
1. "s-h" sounds like?
2. "i" sounds like?
3. "w" sounds like?
4. "w-i-s-h" sounds like?
5. Quickly read the word aloud.

f<u>ish</u>:
1. "s-h" sounds like?
2. "i" sounds like?
3. "f" sounds like?
4. "f-i-s-h" sounds like?
5. Quickly read the word aloud.

Combination "igh" = "i" sound: light, might, right

l<u>igh</u>t:
1. "t" sounds like?
2. "i-g-h" sounds like?
3. "l" sounds like?
4. "l-i-g-h-t" sounds like?
5. Read word quickly.

m<u>igh</u>t:
1. "t" sounds like?
2. "i-g-h" sounds like?
3. "m" sounds like?

      4. "m-i-g-h-t" sounds like?
      5. Quickly read the word aloud.

r<u>igh</u>t: 1. "t" sounds like?
      2. "i-g-h" sounds like?
      3. "r" sounds like?
      4. "r-i-g-h-t" sounds like?
      5. Quickly read the word aloud.

Combination "ild" = long "i" sound: wild, child, mild

w<u>ild</u>:   1. "i-l-d" sounds like?
      2. "w" sounds like?
      3. "w-i-l-d" sounds like?
      4. Quickly read the word aloud

ch<u>ild</u>:   1. "i-l-d" sounds like?
      2. "c-h" sounds like?
      3. "c-h-i-l-d" sounds like?
      4. Quickly read the word aloud.

m<u>ild</u>:   1. "i-l-d" sounds like?
      2. "m" sounds like?
      3. "m-i-l-d" sounds like?
      4. Quickly read the word.

Digraph "aw": lawn, dawn, draw

l<u>aw</u>n: 1. "n" sounds like?
      2. "a-w" sounds like?
      3. "l" sounds like?

                    4. "l-a-w-n" sounds like?
                    5. Quickly read the word aloud.

dr**aw**n: 1. "n" sounds like?
              2. "a-w" sounds like?
              3. "r" sounds like?
              4. "d" sounds like?
              5. "d-r-a-w-n" sounds like?
              6. Quickly read the word aloud.

dr**aw**:   1. "a-w" sounds like?
              2. "r" sounds like?
              3. "d" sounds like?
              4. "d-r-a-w" sounds like?
              5. Quickly read the word aloud.

Combination "ous" = "us" sound: famous, joyous, nervous.

fam**ous**:   1. "o-u-s" sounds like? (**us**).
              2. "m" sounds like?
              3. "a" sounds like?
              4. "f" sounds like?
              5. "f-a-m-o-u-s" sounds like?
              6. Quickly read the word aloud.

joy**ous**:   1. "o-u-s" sounds like?
              2. "o-y" sounds like?
              3. "j" sounds like?
              4. "j-o-y-o-u-s" sounds like?
              5. Quickly read the word aloud.

nerv**ous**:   1. "o-u-s" sounds like?
              2. "v" sounds like?
              3. "e-r" sounds like?
              4. "n" sounds like?

5. "n-e-r-v-o-u-s" sounds like?
6. Quickly read the word aloud.

Digraph "oy": boy, toy, joy

b**oy**:   1. "o-y" sounds like?
               2. "b" sounds like?
               3. "b-o-y" sounds like?
               4. Quickly read the word aloud.

t**oy**:   1. "o-y" sounds like?
               2. "t" sounds like?
               3. "t-o-y" sounds like?
               4. Quickly read the word aloud.

j**oy**:   1. "o-y" sounds like?
               2. "j" sounds like?
               3. "j-o-y" sounds like?
               4. Quickly read the word aloud.

Vowel "a" = "uh" sound: above, afoot, about

above: 1. "e" sounds like?
               2. "v" sounds like?
               3. "o" sounds like?
               4. "b" sounds like?
               5. "a" sounds like?
               6. "a-b-o-v-e "sounds like?
               7. Quickly read the word aloud.

afoot: 1. "t" sounds like?
               2. "o-o" sounds like?
               3. "f" sounds like?

                    4. "a" sounds like?
                    5. "a-f-o-o-t" sounds like?
                    6. Quickly read the word aloud.

about: 1. "t" sounds like?
                    2. "o-u" sounds like?
                    3. "b" sounds like?
                    4. "a" sounds like?
                    5. "a-b-o-u-t" sounds like?
                    6. Quickly read the word aloud.

Blends:

A student must pronounce a long vowel sound and a short vowel sound to hear which phonic version is correct when practicing blends.

    a. Sometimes the "y" has long "*e*" sound (happy) or a long "*i*" sound (my) when it is written at the end of a word. (At other times, the "y" maybe **silent**).

    b. The vowel "a" and "ay" will have a long "a" sound like in the words "bay, day, ray".

Blends "fr": free, fry, freeze, fray, fraud.

free: 1. "e-e" sounds like? (silent).
                    2. "f-r" sounds like?
                    3. "f-r-e-e" sounds like?
                    4. Quickly read the word aloud.

fry:
1. "y" sounds like?
2. "f-r" sounds like?
3. "f-r-y" sounds like?
4. Quickly read the word aloud.

freeze:
1. The last "e" sounds like? (silent).
2. "z" sounds like?
3. "e-e "sounds like?
4. "f-r" sounds like?
5. "f-r-e-e-z-e" sounds like?
6. Quickly read the word aloud.

fr<u>ay</u>:
1. "a-y" sounds like?
2. "f-r" sounds like?
3. "f-r-a-y" sounds like?
4. Quickly read the word aloud.

fr<u>au</u>d:
1. "d" sounds like?
2. "a-u" sounds like? (ah).
3. "f-r" sounds like?
4. "f-r-a-u-d" sounds like?
5. Quickly read the word aloud.

Diphthong Words

A word with vowel letters of "ou" will have several different sounds.

1. s<u>**ou**</u>l = "**ol**" sound

2. tr<u>**ou**</u>t and <u>**out**</u> = "*ow*" sound.

3. s<u>**ou**</u>p = "<u>***ou***</u>" an **open** *oo* sound.

Blend "ou" = "ol" sound: soul, shoulder, boulder

s<u>ou</u>l:
1. "l" sounds like?
2. "o-u" sounds like?
3. "s" sounds like
4. "s-o-u-l" sounds like?
5. Quickly read the word aloud?

sh<u>ou</u>lder:
1. "e-r" sounds like?
3. "d" sounds like?
4. "l" sounds like?
3. "o-u" sounds like?
4. "s-h" sounds like?
5. "s-h-o-u-l-d-e-r" sounds like?
6. Quickly read the word aloud?

b<u>ou</u>lder:
1. "e-r" sounds like?
2. "d" sounds like?
3. "l" sounds like?
4. "o-u" sounds like?
5. "b" sounds like?
6. b-o-u-l-d-e-r sounds like?
7. Quickly read the word aloud.

Diphthong "ou" = "ow" sound: proud, cloud

pr<u>ou</u>d:
1. "d" sounds like?
2. "o-u" sounds like? (ow).
3. "r" sounds like?
4. "p" sounds like?
5. p-r-o-u-d sounds like?
6. Quickly read the word aloud.

cl**ou**d: 1. "d" sounds like?
         2. "o-u" sounds like? (ow).
         3. "l" sounds like?
         4. "c" sounds like?
         5. "c-l-o-u-d" sounds like?
         6. Quickly read the word aloud.

The "**ow**" letters together can have a *long* "**o**" sound and an "**ow**" sound. Moreover, the letters "ow" at the end of a word may have a different sound. If an "**n**" or "**l**" is written before the "ow" letters; You will hear the "ow" sound in words like in "c*l*own." Some words may **not** have the "**n**" or "**l**". Notice "**cow**" has the same sound as "cl**ow**n," but cow has no "n" or "l" letter prior to "ow."

Diphthong "ow" = long "o" sound: grow, own

gr**ow**: 1. "o-w" sounds like?
         2. "r" sounds like?
         3. "g" sounds like?
         4. "g-r-o-w" sounds like?
         5. Quickly read the word aloud.

own: 1. "n" sounds like?
         2. "o-w" sounds like? (silent).
         3. "o-w-n" sounds like?
         4. Quickly read the word aloud.

Diphthong "ow" = short "o" sound: now, down

n**ow**: 1. "o-w" sounds like?
         2. "n" sounds like?

                  3. "n-o-w" sounds like?
                  4. Quickly say the word aloud.

d<u>ow</u>n: 1. "n" sounds like?
              2. "o-w" sounds like?
              3. "d" sounds like?
              4. "d-o-w-n" sounds like?
              5. Quickly read the word aloud.

"dr" blend: drive, drip, drill

<u>dr</u>ive: 1. "e" sounds like?
              2. "v" sounds like?
              3. "i" sounds like?
              4. "d-r" sounds like?
              6. "d-r-i-v-e" sounds like?
              7. Quickly read the word aloud.

<u>dr</u>ip: 1. "p" sounds like?
              2. "i" sounds like?
              3. "d-r" sounds like?
              4. "d-r-i-p" sounds like?
              5. Quickly read the word aloud.

<u>dr</u>ill   1. "l-l" sounds like?
              2. "i" sounds like?
              3. "d-r" sounds like?
              4. "d-r-i-l-l" sounds like?
              5. Quickly read the word aloud.

Blend "fl": flip, flop, flap.

<u>fl</u>ip: 1. "p" sounds like?
              2. "i" sounds like?
              3. "f-l" sounds like?

                4. "f-l-i-p" sounds like?
                5. Quickly read the word aloud.

flop:
1. "p" sounds like?
2. "o" sounds like?
3. "f-l" sounds like?
4. "f-l-o-p" sounds like?
5. Read word quickly.

flap:
1. "p" sounds like?
2. "a" sounds like?
3. "f-l" sounds like?
4. "f-l-a-p" sounds like?
5. Quickly read the word aloud.

Blend "bl": bliss, bless, blaze

bliss:
1. "s-s" sounds like?
2. "i" sounds like?
3. "b-l" sounds like?
4. "b-l-i-s-s" sounds like?
5. Quickly read the word aloud.

bless:
1. "s-s" sounds like?
2. "e" sounds like?
3. "b-l" sounds like?
4. "b-l-e-s-s" sounds like?
5. Quickly read the word aloud.

blaze:
1. "e" sounds like?
2. "z" sounds like?
3. "a" sounds like?
4. "b-l" sounds like?
5. "b-l-a-z-e" sounds like? Quickly read the word aloud.

Blend "cr": across, crumb, creek

a**cr**oss:
1. "s-s" sounds like?
2. "o" sounds like?
3. "c-r" sounds like?
4. "a" sounds like?
5. "a-c-r-o-s-s" sounds like?
6. Quickly read the word aloud.

crumb:
1. "b" sounds like? (silent)
2. "m" sounds like?
3. "u" sounds like?
4. "c-r" sounds like?
5. "c-r-u-m-b" sounds like?
6. Quickly read the word aloud.

creek:
1. "k" sounds like?
2. "e-e" sounds like?
3. "c-r" sounds like?
4. "c-r-e-e-k" sounds like?
5. Quickly read the word aloud.

The "gh" is a ***digraph*** that has another sound when it starts a word. The letter "gh can be found in the middle of longer words (spaghetti). The letters "gh" have one sound. For example: **gh**ost, **gh**etto, **gh**aff.

ghost:
1. "t" sounds like?
2. "s" sounds like?
3. "o" sounds like?
4. "g-h" sounds like?
5. "g-h-o-s-t" sounds like?
6. Quickly read the word aloud.

ghetto: 1. "o" sounds like?
2. "t-t" sounds like?
3. "e" sounds like?
4. "g-h" sounds like?
5. "g-h-e-t-t-o" sounds like?
6. Quickly read the word aloud.

ghaff: 1. "f-f" sounds like?
2. "a" sounds like?
3. "g-h" sounds like?
4. "g-h-a-f-f?" sounds like?
5. Quickly read the word aloud.

Blend "gr": green, grant, grumpy.

green: 1. "n" sounds like?
2. "e-e" sounds like?
3. "g-r" sounds like?
4. "g-r-e-e-n" sounds like?
5. Quickly read the word aloud
6. What is another name for "gr"? (**blend**)

grant: 1. "t" sounds like?
2. "n" sounds like?
3. "a" sounds like?
4. "g-r" sounds like?
5. "g-r-a-n-t" sounds like?
6. Quickly read the word aloud.

grumpy:
1. "y" sounds like?
2. "p" sounds like?
3. "m" sounds like?
4. "u" sounds like?
5. "g-r" sounds like?
6. "g-r-u-m-p-y" sounds like?
7. Quickly read the word aloud.

Blend "cl": cliff, cloud, claim.

cliff:
1. "f-f" sounds like?
2. "i" sounds like?
3. "c-l" sounds like?
4. "c-l-i-f-f" sounds like?
5. Quickly read the word aloud.

cloud:
1. "d" sounds like?
2. "o-u" sounds like?
3. "c-l" sounds like?
4. "c-l-o-u-d" sounds like?
5. Quickly read the word aloud.
6. Another name for "o-u"? **(diphthong)**

claim:
1. "m" sounds like?
2. "i" sounds like? **(silent)**.
3. "a" sound like?
4. "c-l" sounds like?
5. "c-l-a-i-m" sound like?
6. Quickly read the word aloud.

Blend "pl": plate, play, plant.

plate:
1. "e" sounds like?
2. "t" sounds like?

                    3. "a" sounds like?
                    4. "p-l" sounds like?
                    5. "p-l-a-t-e" sound like?
                    6. Quickly read the word aloud.

play: 1. "y" sounds like?
                    2. "a" sounds like?
                    3. "p-l" sounds like?
                    4. "p-l-a-y" sound like?
                    5. Quickly read the word aloud

plant: 1. "t" sounds like?
                    2. "n" sounds like?
                    3. "a" sounds like?
                    4. "p-l" sounds like?
                    5. "p-l-a-n-t" sounds like?
                    6. Quickly read the word aloud.

Blend "pr": pride, proud, prime.

pride: 1. "e" sounds like?
                    2. "d" sounds like?
                    3. "i" sounds like?
                    4. "p-r" sounds like?
                    5. "p-r-i-d-e" sounds like?
                    6. Quickly read the word aloud.

proud: 1. "d" sounds like?
                    2. "o-u" sounds like?
                    3. "p-r" sounds like?
                    4. "p-r-o-u-d" sounds like?
                    5. Quickly read the word aloud.

prime: 1. "e" sounds like?
                    2. "m" sounds like?

3. "i" sounds like?
4. "p-r" sounds like?
5. "p-r-i-m-e" sounds like?
6. Quickly read the word aloud.

Blend "sc": scout, scare, scream.

scout:
1. "t" sounds like?
2. "o-u" sounds like?
3. "s-c" sounds like?
4. "s-c-o-u-t" sounds like?
5. Quickly read the word aloud.

scare:
1. "e" sounds like?
2. "a-r" sounds like? (air).
3. "s-c" sounds like?
4. "s-c-a-r-e" sound like?
5. Quickly read the word aloud.

scream:
1. "m" sounds like?
2 "e-a" sounds like?
3. "r" sounds like?
4. "s-c" sounds like?
5. "s-c-r-e-a-m" sounds like?
6. Quickly read the word aloud.

Blend "sk": skip, skill, brisk

skip:
1. "p" sounds like?
2. "i" sounds like?
3. "s-k" sounds like?
4. "s-k-i-p" sounds like?
5. Quickly read the word aloud.

skill: 1. "l-l" sounds like?
       2. "i" sounds like?
       3. "s-k" sounds like?
       4. "s-k-i-l-l" sounds like?
       5. Quickly read the word aloud.

bri**sk**:   1. "s-k" sounds like?
       2. "i" sounds like?
       3. "r" sounds like?
       4. "b" sounds like?
       5. "b-r-i-s-k" sounds like?
       6. Quickly read the word aloud.

Blend "sl": slow, slide, sled.

slow: 1. "w" sounds like? (**silent**).
       2. "o" sounds like?
       3. "s-l" sounds like?
       4. "s-l-o-w" sounds like?
       5. Quickly read the word aloud.

slide: 1. "e" sounds like?
       2. "d" sounds like?
       3. "i" sounds like?
       4. "s-l" sounds like?
       5. "s-l-i-d-e" sounds like?
       6. Quickly read the word aloud.

sled: 1. "d" sounds like?
       2. "e" sounds like?
       3. "s-l" sounds like?
       4. "s-l-e-d" sounds like?
       5. Quickly read the word aloud.

Blend "sm": small, smile, smart

<u>sm</u>all:
1. "l-l" sounds like?
2. "a" sounds like?
3. "s-m" sounds like?
4. "s-m-a-l-l" sounds like?
5. Quickly read the word aloud.

<u>sm</u>ile:
1. "e" sounds like?
2. "l" sounds like?
3. "i" sounds like?
4. "s-m" sounds like?
5. "s-m-i-l-e" sounds like?
6. Quickly read the word aloud.

<u>sm</u>art:
1. "t" sounds like?
2. "r" sounds like?
3. "a" sounds like?
4. "s-m" sounds like?
5. "s-m-a-r-t" sounds like?
6. Quickly read the word aloud.

Blend "sn": snare, snail, snack

<u>sn</u>are:
1. "e" sounds like? **(silent).**
2. "r" sounds like?
3. "a" sounds like?
4. "a-r" together sounds like? **(air).**
5. "s-n" sounds like?
6. "s-n-a-r-e" sound like?
7. Quickly read the word aloud.
8. What two letters are blends? **(S-N)**

snail:
1. "l" sounds like?
2. "i" sounds like?
3. "a" sounds like?
4. "s-n" sounds like?
5. "s-n-a-i-l" sounds like?
6. Quickly read the word aloud.

snack:
1. "c-k" sounds like?
2. "a" sounds like?
3. "s-n" sounds like?
4. "s-n-a-c-k" sounds like?
5. Quickly read the word aloud.

Blend "sp": spoke, speak, spend.

spoke:
1. "e" sounds like?
2. "k" sounds like?
3. "o" sounds like?
4. "s-p" sounds like?
5. "s-p-o-k-e" sounds like?
6. Quickly read the word aloud.

speak:
1. "k" sounds like?
2. "e-a" sounds like?
3. "s-p" sounds like?
4. "s-p-e-a-k" sounds like?
5. Quickly read the word aloud.
6. What's the rule on two vowels together? **(First vowel is heard)**

spend:
1. "d" sounds like?
2. "n" sounds like?
3. "e" sounds like?
4. "s-p" sounds like?

5. "s-p-e-n-d" sounds like?
6. Quickly read the word aloud.

Blend "st": star, stoop, stop.

star:
1. "a-r" sounds like?
2. "s-t" sounds like?
3. "s-t-a-r" sounds like?
4. Quickly read the word aloud.

stoop:
1. "p" sounds like?
2. "o-o" sounds like?
3. "s-t" sounds like?
4. "s-t-o-o-p" sounds like?
5. Quickly read the word aloud.

stop:
1. "p" sounds like?
2. "o" sounds like?
3. "s-t" sounds like?
4. "s-t-o-p" sounds like?
5. Quickly read the word aloud.

Blend "sw": swell, swing, swim

swell:
1. "l-l" sounds like?
2. "e" sounds like?
3. "s-w" sounds like?
4. "s-w-e-l-l" sound like
5. Quickly read the word aloud.

swing:
1. "g" sounds like?
2. "n" sounds like?
3. "i" sounds like?

	4. "s-w" sounds like?
	5. "s-w-i-n-g" sounds like?
	6. Quickly read the word aloud.

swim:	1. "m" sounds like?
	2. "i" sounds like?
	3. "s-w" sounds like?
	4. "s-w-i-m" sounds like?
	5. Quickly read the words aloud.

Blend "tr": trade, trap, trip

trade:	1. "e" sounds like? **(silent)**
	2. "d" sounds like?
	3. "a" sounds like?
	4. "t-r" sounds like?
	5. "t-r-a-de" sound like?
	6. Quickly read the word aloud.

trap:	1. "p" sounds like?
	2. "a" sounds like?
	3. "t-r" sounds like?
	4. "t-r-a-p" sounds like?
	5. Quickly read the word aloud.

Blend "tw": twine, twin, twig

twine:	1. "e" sounds like?
	2. "n" sounds like?
	3. "i" sounds like?
	4. "t-w" sounds like?
	5. "t-w-i-n-e" sounds like?
	6. Quickly read the word aloud.

twin:
    1. "n" sounds like?
    2. "i" sounds like?
    3. "t-w" sounds like?
    4. "t-w-i-n" sounds like?
    5. Quickly read the word aloud.

twig:
    1. "g" sounds like?
    2. "i" sounds like?
    3. "t-w" sounds like?
    4. "t-w-i-g" sounds like?
    5. Quickly read the word aloud.

Digraphs have one sound and two consonant letters. They do not change their sounds. Consonants never change their sound, but vowels will change their sound.

Digraph "sh": shed, shame, cash rush, shush, mush.

shed:
    1. "d" sounds like?
    2. "e" sounds like?
    3. "s-h" sounds like?
    4. "s-h-e-d" sounds like?
    5. Quickly read the word aloud.

shame:
    1. "e" sounds like?
    2. "m" sounds like?
    3. "a" sounds like?
    4. "s-h" sounds like?
    5. "s-h-a-m-e" sounds like?
    6. Quickly read the word aloud.

ca**sh**:
1. "s-h" sounds like?
2. "a" sounds like?
3. "c" sounds like?
4. "c-a-s-h" sounds like?
5. Quickly read the word aloud.
6. Another name for "s-h"? **(digraph)**

ru**sh**:
1. "s-h" sounds like?
2. "u" sounds like?
3. "r" sounds like?
4. "r-u-s-h" sounds like?
5. Quickly read the word aloud.

mu**sh**:
1. "s-h" sounds like?
2. "u" sounds like?
3. "m" sounds like?
4. "m-u-s-h" sounds like?
5. Quickly read the word aloud.

shu**sh**:
1. "s-h" ending sounds like?
2. "u" sounds like?
3. "s-h" beginning sounds like?
4. "s-h-u-s-h" sounds like?
5. Quickly read the word aloud.

Place a finger or two on the throat to hear and to feel the closed or open sound of a word as it is pronounced.

Blend "ew" = "oo" closed sound: jewel, crew, few.

j**ew**el:
1. "l" sounds like?
2. "e" sounds like?
3. "e-w" sounds like?

4. "j" sounds like?
5. "j-e-w-e-l" sounds like? Quickly read the word aloud

cr**ew**:
1. "e-w" sounds like?
2. "r" sounds like?
3. "c" sounds like?
4. "c-r-e-w" sounds like?
5. Quietly read the word aloud.

f**ew**:
1. "e-w" sounds like?
2. "f" sounds like?
3. "f-e-w" sounds like?
4. Quickly read the word aloud.

Combination "ind"=Short I sound: bind, mind, blind.

b***ind***:
1. "d" sounds like?
2. "n" sounds like?
3. "i" sounds like?
4. "b" sounds like?
5. "b-i-n-d" sounds likes? Quickly read the word aloud.

m***ind***:
1. "d" sounds like?
2. "n" sounds like?
3. "i" sounds like?
4. "m" sounds like?
5. "m-i-n-d" sounds like? Quickly read the word aloud.

bl***ind***:
1. "d" sounds like?
2. "n" sounds like?
3. "i" sounds like?
4. "l" sounds like?
5. "b" sounds like?
6. "b-l-i-n-d" sounds like? Quickly read the word aloud.

Blend "ic" sound: sick, tickle, musical.

s<u>ic</u>k:
1. "c-k" sounds like?
2. "i" sounds like?
3. "s" sounds like?
4. "s-i-c-k" sounds like?
5. Quickly read the word aloud.

t<u>ic</u>kle:
1. "e" sounds like?
2. "l" sounds like?
3. "c-k" sounds like?
4. "i" sounds like?
5. "t" sounds like?
6. "t-i-c-k-l-e" sounds like?
7. Quickly read the word aloud.

mus<u>ic</u>al:
1. "l" sounds like?
2. "a" sounds like?
3. "i-c" sounds like?
4. "u" sounds like?
5. "m" sounds like?
6. "m-u-s-i-c-a-l" sounds like?
7. Quickly read the word aloud.

Digraph "wr" = "r" sound: wrap, wrong, wrote

<u>wr</u>ap:
1. "p" sounds like?
2. "a" sounds like?
3. "w-r" sounds like?
4. "w-r-a-p" sounds like?
5. Quickly read the word aloud.

wrong:
1. "g" sounds like?
2. "n" sounds like?
3. "o" sounds like?
4. "w-r" sounds like?
5. "w-r-o-n-g" sounds like?
6. Quickly read the word aloud.

wrote:
1. "e" sounds like?
2. "t" sounds like?
3. "o" sounds like?
4. "w-r" sounds like?
5. "w-r-o-t-e" sounds like?
6. Quickly read the word aloud.

Blend "ng": long, spring, ring.

lo**ng**:
1. "n-g" sounds like?
2. "o" sounds like?
3. "l" sounds like?
4. "l-o-n-g" sounds like?
5. Quickly read the word aloud.

spri**ng**:
1. "n-g" sounds like?
2. "i" sounds like?
3. "r" sounds like
4. "p" sounds like?
5. "s" sounds like?
6. "s-p-r-i-n-g" sounds like?
7. Quickly read the word aloud.

ri**ng**: 1. "n-g" sounds like?
2. "i" sounds like?
3. "r" sounds like?
4. "r-i-n-g" sounds like?
5. Quickly read the word aloud.

Digraph "ck" = "k" sound: kick, thick, clock

ki**ck**: 1. "c-k" sounds like?
2. "i" sounds like?
3. "k" sounds like?
4. "k-i-c-k" sounds like?
5. Quickly read the word aloud.

thi**ck**: 1. "c-k" sounds like?
2. "i" sounds like?
3. "t-h" sounds like?
4. "t-h-i-c-k" sounds like?
5. Quickly read the word aloud.

clo**ck**: 1. "c-k" sounds like?
2. "o" sounds like?
3. "l" sounds like?
4. "c" sounds like?
5. "c-l-o-c-k" sounds like?
6. Quickly read the word aloud.

Consonant "k": keep, kind, Kenny.

keep: 1. "p" sounds like?
3. "e-e" sounds like?
4. "k" sounds like?

5. "k-e-e-p" sounds like? Quickly read the word aloud.

kind:
1. "d" sounds like?
2. "n" sounds like?
3. "i" sounds like?
4. "k" sounds like?
5. "k-i-n-d" sounds like? Quickly read the word aloud.

Kenny:
1. "y" sounds like?
2. "n-n" sounds like?
3. "e" sounds like?
4. "k" sounds like?
5. "K-e-n-n-y" sounds like?
6. Quickly read the word aloud.

Blend "kn" = "n" sound ("k" is silent): know, knot, knock.

know:
1. "w" sounds like?
2. "o" sounds like?
3. "k-n" sounds like?
4. "k-n-o-w" sounds like?
5. Quickly read the word aloud.

knot:
1. "t" sounds like?
2. "o" sounds like?
3. "k-n" sounds like?
4. "k-n-o-t" sounds like?
5. Quickly read the word aloud.

knock:
1. "c-k" sounds like?
2. "o" sounds like?

    3. "k-n" sounds like?
    4. "k-n-o-c-k" sounds like?
    5. Quickly read the word aloud.

Vowel long "i": ice, rice, kite.

i̱ce: 1. "e" sounds like?
    2. "c" sounds like?
    3. "i" sounds like?
    4. "i-c-e sounds like?
    5. Quickly read the word aloud
    6. Long vowel sounds say what? (**Their names**)

ri̱ce: 1. "e" sounds like?
    2. "c" sounds like?
    3. "i" sounds like?
    4. "r" sounds like?
    5. "r-i-c-e" sounds like?
    6. Quickly read the word aloud.

ki̱te: 1. "e" sounds like?
    2. "t" sounds like?
    3. "i" sounds like?
    4. "k" sounds like?
    5. "k-i-t-e" sounds like?
    6. Quickly read the word aloud.

Vowel short "i": tin, win, sin

ti̱n: 1. "n" sounds like?
    2. "i" sounds like?
    3. "t" sounds like?
    4. "t-i-n" sounds like? Quickly read the word aloud.

w<u>i</u>n: 1. "n" sounds like?
2. "i" sounds like?
3. "w" sounds like?
4. "w-i-n" sounds like?
5. Quickly read the word aloud.

s<u>i</u>n: 1. "n" sounds like?
2. "i" sounds like?
3. "s" sounds like?
4. "s-i-n" sounds like?
5. Quickly read the word aloud?

Blend "im" = short "i" sound: dim, slim, him

d<u>im</u>: 1. "i-m" sounds like?
2. "d" sounds like?
3. "d-i-m" sounds like?
4. Quickly read the word aloud.

sl<u>im</u>: 1. "i-m" sounds like?
2. "l" sounds like?
3. "s" sounds like?
4. "s-l-i-m" sounds like?
5. Quickly read the word aloud.

h<u>im</u>: 1. "i-m" sounds like?
2. "h" sounds like?
3. "h-i-m" sounds like?
4. Quickly read the word aloud.

Blend "um": sum, stump, drums.

s**um**:   1. "u-m" sounds like?
               2. "s" sounds like?
               3. "s-u-m" sounds like?
               4. Quickly read the word aloud.

st**um**p: 1. "p" sounds like?
               2. "u-m" sounds like?
               3. "t" sounds like?
               4. "s" sounds like?
               5. "s-t-u-m-p" sounds like?
               6. Quickly read the word aloud.

dr**um**s: 1. "s" sounds like?
               2. "u-m" sounds like?
               3. "r" sounds like?
               4. "d" sounds like?
               5. "d-r-u-m-s" sounds like?
               6. Quickly read the word aloud

Blend "ing" =short "i" sound: wing, sing, ring, king, swing.

w*ing*:   1. "i-n-g" sounds like?
               2. "w" sounds like?
               3. "w-i-n-g" sounds like?
               4. Quickly read the word aloud.

s*ing*:   1. "i-n-g" sounds like?
               2. "s" sounds like?
               3. "s-i-n-g" sounds like?
               4. Quickly read the word aloud.

r*ing*   1. "i-n-g" sounds like?
               2. "r" sounds like?

                3. "r-i-n-g" sounds like?
                4. Quickly read the word aloud.

k*in*g: 1. "i-n-g" sounds like?
                2. "k" sounds like?
                3. "k-i-n-g" sounds like?
                4. Quickly read the word aloud.

sw*in*g: 1. "i-n-g" sounds like?
                2. "w" sounds like?
                3. "s" sounds like?
                4. "s-w-i-n-g" sounds like?
                5. Quickly read the word aloud.

Consonant "s" = "z" sound: cheese, days, does.

chee*s*e: 1. "e" sounds like?
                2. "s" sounds like? (**"z"**)
                3. "e-e" sounds like?
                4. "c-h" sounds like?
                5. "c-h-e-e-s-e" sounds like?
                6. Quickly read the word aloud.

day*s*:   1. "s" sounds like?
                2. "y" sounds like?
                3. "a" sounds like?
                4. "d" sounds like?
                5. "d-a-y-s" sounds like?
                6. Quickly read the word aloud.

doe*s*:   1. "s" sound like?
                2. "e" sounds like?
                3. "o" sounds like?
                4. "d" sounds like?

        5. "d-o-e-s" sounds like?
        6. Quickly read the word aloud.

Blend "qu" = "kw" sound: quick, quiet, quiz.

quick:
1. "c-k" sounds like?
2. "i" sounds like?
3. "q-u" sounds like?
4. "q-u-i-c-k" sound like? Quickly read the word aloud.

quiet:
1. "t" sounds like?
2. "e" sounds like?
3. "i" sounds like?
4. "q-u" sounds like?
5. "q-u-i-e-t" sounds like?
6. Quickly read the word aloud.

quiz:
1. "z" sounds like?
2. "i" sounds like?
3. "q-u" sounds like?
4. "q-u-i-z" sounds like?
5. Quickly read the word aloud.

Digraph "ch": hatch, patch, watch.

hat**ch**:
1. "c-h" sounds like?
2. "t" sounds like?
3. "a" sounds like?
4. "h" sounds like?
5. "h-a-t-c-h" sounds like?
6. Quickly read the word aloud.
7. Another name for "c-h" letters? **(digraph)**

pa**tch**:
1. "c-h" sounds like?
2. "t" sounds like?
3. "a" sounds like?
4. "p" sounds like?
5. "p-a-t-c-h" sounds like?
6. Quickly read the word aloud.

wa**tch**:
1. "c-h" sounds like?
2. "t" sounds like?
3. "a" sounds like?
4. "w" sounds like?
5. "w-a-t-c-h" sounds like?
6. Quickly read the word aloud.

Digraph "ck": back, rack, pack.

ba**ck**:
1. "c-k" sounds like?
2. "a" sounds like?
3. "b" sounds like?
3. "b-a-c-k" sounds like?
4. Quickly read the word aloud.

ra**ck**:
1. "c-k" sounds like?
2. "a" sounds like?
3. "r" sounds like?
4. "r-a-c-k" sounds like?
5. Quickly read the word aloud.

pa**ck**:
1. "c-k" sounds like?
2. "a" sounds like?
3. "p" sounds like?
3. "p-a-c-k" sounds like?
4. Quickly read the word aloud.

Blend "op": top, mop, stop.

t<u>op</u>:
1. "o-p" sounds like?
2. "t" sounds like?
3. "t-o-p" sounds like?
4. Quickly read the word aloud.

m<u>op</u>:
1. "o-p" sounds like?
2. "m" sounds like?
3. "m-o-p" sounds like?
4. Quickly read the word aloud.

st<u>op</u>:
1. "o-p" sounds like?
2. "t" sounds like?
3. "s" sounds like?
4. "s-t-o-p" sounds like?
5. Quickly read the word aloud.

Long "o" one syllable words: tone, drone, phone.

t<u>o</u>ne:
1. "e" sounds like?
2. "n" sounds like?
3. "o" sounds like?
4. "t" sounds like?
5. "t-o-n-e" sounds like?
6. Quickly read the word aloud.

dr<u>o</u>ne:
1. "e" sounds like?
2. "n" sounds like?
3. "o" sounds like?
4. "r" sounds like?
5. "d" sounds like?
6. "d-r-o-n-e" sounds like?
7. Quickly read the word aloud.

ph**o**ne: 1. "e" sounds like?
2. "n" sounds like?
3. "o" sounds like?
4. "p-h" sounds like?
5. "p-h-o-n-e" sounds like?
6. Quickly read the word aloud.

"es" = short "e" with a double "s-s": bless, lesson, chess.

bl**es**s: 1. "s-s" sounds like?
2. "e" sounds like?
3. "l" sounds like?
4. "b" sounds like?
5. "b-l-e-s-s" sounds like? Quickly read the word aloud.

l**es**son: 1. "n" sounds like?
2. "o" sounds like?
3. "s-s" sounds like?
4. "e" sounds like?
5. "l" sounds like?
6. "l-e-s-s-o-n" sounds like? Quickly read the word aloud.

ch**es**s: 1. "s-s" sounds like?
2. "e" sounds like?
3. "c-h" sounds like?
4. "c-h-e-s-s" sounds like? Quickly read the word aloud.

"eck" = short "e" sound: neck, deck, peck.
Ask students which letters are a digraph in the following words.

n**eck**: 1. "c-k" sounds like?
2. "e" sounds like?
3. "n" sounds like?
4. "n-e-c-k" sounds like?
5. Quickly read the word aloud.

d**eck**:
1. "c-k" sounds like?
2. "e" sounds like?
3. "d" sounds like?
4. "d-e-c-k" sounds like?
5. Quickly read the word aloud.

p**eck**:
1. "c-k" sounds like?
2. "e" sounds like?
3. "p" sounds like?
4. "p-e-c-k" sounds like? Quickly read the word aloud.

Bland "as" = short "a" sound: brass, grass, passing.

br**ass**:
1. "s-s" sounds like?
2. "a" sounds like?
3. "r" sounds like?
4. "b" sounds like?
5. "b-r-a-s-s" sounds like?
6. Quickly read the word aloud.

gr**ass**:
1. "s-s" sounds like?
2. "a" sounds like?
3. "r" sounds like?
4. "g" sounds like?
5. "g-r-a-s-s" sounds like?
6. Quickly read the word aloud.

pa**ss**ing:
1. "i-n-g" sounds like?
2. "s-s" sounds like?
3. "a" sounds like?
4. "p" sounds like?
5. "p-a-s-s-i-n-g" sounds like?
6. Quickly read the word aloud.

"ore" words: score, snore, shore.

sc**ore**:
1. "o-r-e" sounds like?
3. "c" sounds like?
4. "s" sounds like?
5. "s-c-o-r-e" sounds like?
6. Quickly read the word aloud.

sn**ore**:
1. "o-r-e" sounds like?
2. "n" sounds like?
3. "s" sounds like?
4. "s-n-o-r-e" sounds like?
5. Quickly read the word aloud.

sh**ore**:
1. "o-r-e" sounds like?
3. "s-h" sounds like?
4. "s-h-o-r-e "sounds like?
5. Quickly read the word aloud.

"ost" = long "o" sound: host, most, post.

h**ost**:
1. "o-s-t" sounds like?
2. "h" sounds like?
3. "h-o-s-t" sounds like?
4. Quickly read the word aloud.

m**ost**:
1. "o-s-t" sounds like?
2. "m" sounds like?
3. "m-o-s-t" sounds like?
4. Quickly read the word aloud.

p**ost**:
1. "o-s-t" sounds like?
2. "p" sounds like?
3. "p-o-s-t" sounds like?
4. Quickly read the word aloud.

Blend "el" words: held, elm, elder

h**el**d:
1. "d" sounds like?
2. "e-l" sounds like?
3. "h" sounds like?
4. "h-e-l-d" sounds like?
5. Quickly read the word aloud.

elm:
1. "m" sounds like?
2. "e-l' sounds like?
3. "e-l-m" sounds like?
4. Quickly read the word aloud.

elder:
1. "e-r" sounds like?
2. "d" sounds like?
3. "e-l" sounds like?
4. "e-l-d-e-r" sounds like?
5. Quickly read the word aloud.

Blend "op" words: top, slop, stop.

t**op**:
1. "o-p" sounds like?
2. "t" sounds like?
3. "t-o-p" sounds like?
4. Quickly read the word aloud.

sl**op**:
1. "o-p" sounds like?
2. "l" sounds like?
3. "s" sounds like?
4. "s-l-o-p" sounds like?
5. Quickly read the word aloud.

st**op**: 1. "o-p" sounds like?
2. "t" sounds like?
3. "s" sounds like?
4. "s-t-o-p" sounds like?
5. Quickly read the word aloud.

Blend "ot" words: got, not, hot

g**ot**: 1. "o-t" sounds like?
2. "g" sounds like?
3. "g-o-t" sounds like?
4. Quickly read the word aloud.

n**ot**: 1. "o-t" sounds like?
2. "n" sounds like?
3. "n-o-t" sounds like?
4. Quickly read the word aloud.

h**ot**: 1. "o-t" sounds like?
2. "h" sounds like?
3. "h-o-t" sounds like?
4. Quickly read the word aloud.

Blend "and" words: land, stand, band.

l**and**: 1. "a-n-d" sounds like?
2. "l" sounds like?
3. "l-a-n-d" sounds like?
4. Quickly read the word aloud.

st**and**:   1. "a-n-d" sounds like?
                 2. "t" sounds like?
                 3. "s" sounds like?
                 4. "s-t-a-n-d" sounds like?
                 5. Quickly read the word aloud.

b**and**:   1. "a-n-d" sounds like?
                 2. "b" sounds like?
                 3. "b-a-n-d" sounds like?
                 4. Quickly read the word aloud.

Blend "ap" words = short "a" sound: map, flap, gap.

m*ap*:   1. "a-p" sounds like?
                 3. "m" sounds like?
                 4. "m-a-p "sounds like?
                 5. Quickly read the word aloud.

fl*ap*:   1. "a-p" sounds like?
                 2. "l" sounds like?
                 3. "f" sounds like?
                 4. "f-l-a-p" sounds like?
                 5. Quickly read the word aloud.

g*ap*:   1. "a-p" sounds like?
                 2. "g" sounds like?
                 3. "g-a-p" sounds like?
                 4. Quickly read the word aloud.

Blend "old" words = long "o" sound: gold, cold, told

g*old*:   1. "o-l-d" sounds like?
                 2. "g" sounds like?
                 3. "g-o-l-d" sounds like?
                 4. Quickly read the word aloud.

c**o**ld: 1. "o-l-d" sounds like?
2. "c" sounds like?
3. "c-o-l-d" sounds like?
4. Quickly read the word aloud.

t**o**ld: 1. "o-l-d" sounds like?
2. "t" sounds like?
3. "t-o-l-d" sounds like?
4. Quickly read the word aloud.

Blend "ab" words = short "a" sound: tab, crab, cab.

t**a**b: 1. "a-b" sounds like?
2. "t" sounds like?
3. "t-a-b" sounds like?
4. Quickly read the word aloud.

cr**a**b: 1. "a-b" sounds like?
2. "r" sounds like?
3. "c" sounds like?
4. "c-r-a-b" sounds like?
5. Quickly read the word aloud.

c**a**b: 1. "a-b" sounds like?
2. "c" sounds like?
3. "c-a-b" sounds like?
4. Quickly read the word aloud.

Blend "ag" words = short "a" sound: flag, drag, tag.

fl**a**g: 1. "a-g" sounds like?
3. "l" sounds like?
4. "f" sounds like?
5. "f-l-a-g" sounds like?
6. Quickly read the word aloud.

dr**ag**:   1. "a-g" sounds like?
              2. "r" sounds like?
              3. "d" sounds like?
              4. "d-r-a-g" sounds like?
              5. Quickly read the word aloud.

t**ag**:   1. "a-g" sounds like?
              2. "t" sounds like?
              3. "t-a-g" sounds like?
              4. Quickly read the word aloud.

Blend "ou" = "ow" sound: out & found.

out: 1. "t" sounds like?
              2. "o-u" sounds like?
              3. "o-u-t" sounds like?
              4. Quickly read the word aloud.

f**ou**nd: 1. "d" sounds like?
              2. "n" sounds like?
              3. "o-u" sounds like?
              4. "f" sounds like?
              5. "f-o-u-n-d" sounds like?
              6. Quickly read the word aloud.

Short "a" words: jam, Sam, ham

j**a**m: 1. "m" sounds like?
              2. "a" sounds like?
              3. "j" sounds like?
              4. "j-a-m" sounds like?
              5. Quickly read the word aloud.

S**a**m: 1. "m" sounds like?
            2. "a" sounds like?
            3. "s" sounds like?
            4. "S-a-m" sounds like?
            5. Quickly read the word aloud.

h**a**m: 1. "m" sounds like?
            2. "a" sounds like?
            3. "h" sounds like?
            4. "h-a-m" sounds like?
            5. Quickly read the word aloud.

Blend "ash" words = short "a" sound: dash, cash, crash.

d**ash**:   1. "a-s-h" sounds like?
            2. "d" sounds like?
            3. "d-a-s-h" sounds like?
            4. Quickly read the word aloud.
            5. What is another name for "s-h"? (**digraph**)

c**ash**:   1. "a-s-h" sounds like?
            2. "c" sounds like?
            3. "c-a-s-h" sounds like?
            4. Quickly read the word aloud.

cr**ash**:   1. "a-s-h" sounds like?
            2. "r" sounds like?
            3. "c" sounds like?
            4. "c-r-a-s-h" sounds like?
            5. Quickly read the word aloud.

Blend "ish" words = short "i" sound: dish, wish, foolish.

d*ish*: 1. "i-s-h" sounds like?
        2. "d" sounds like?
        3. "d-i-s-h" sounds like?
        4. Quickly read the word aloud.

w*ish*: 1. "i-s-h" sounds like?
        2. "w" sounds like?
        3. "w-i-s-h" sounds like?
        4. Quickly read the word aloud.

fool*ish*: 1. "i-s-h" sounds like?
        2. "l" sounds like?
        3. "o-o" sounds like?
        4. "f" sounds like?
        5. "f-o-o-l-i-s-h" sounds like?
        6. Quickly read the word aloud.

Blend "eam" words = long "e" sound: team, cream, beam.

t*eam*: 1. "e-a-m" sounds like?
        2. "t" sounds like?
        3. "t-e-a-m" sounds like?
        4. Quickly read the word aloud.

cr*eam*: 1. "e-a-m" sounds like?
        2. "r" sounds like?
        3. "c" sounds like?
        4. "c-r-e-a-m" sounds like?
        5. Quickly read the word aloud.

b**ea**m: 1. "e-a-m" sounds like?
              4. "b" sounds like?
              5. "b-e-a-m" sounds like?
              6. Quickly read the word aloud.

Blend "ave" = long "a" vowel with silent "e" words: cave, save, behave.

The letter "e" at the end of a word makes the vowel say its name sound.

c***ave***:   1. "a-v-e" sounds like?
             2. "c" sounds like?
             3. "c-a-v-e" sounds like?
             4. Quickly read the word aloud.

s***ave***:   1. "a-v-e" sounds like?
             2. "s" sounds like?
             3. "s-a-v-e" sounds like?
             4. Quickly read the word aloud

beh***ave***:   1. "a-v-e" sounds like?
              2. "h" sounds like?
              3. "e" sounds like?
              4. "b" sounds like?
              5. "b-e-h-a-v-e" sounds like?
              6. Quickly read the word aloud.

Blend "ove" words = long "o" sound: over, grove, dove.

***o**ve*r: 1. "r" sounds like?
             2. "o-v-e" sounds like?
             3. "o-v-e-r" sounds like?
             4. Quickly read the word aloud.

gr***ove***:   1. "o-v-e" sounds like?
                2. "r" sounds like?
                3. "g" sounds like?
                4. "g-r-o-v-e" sounds like?
                5. Quickly read the word aloud.

d***ove***:   1. "o-v-e" sounds like?
                2. "d" sounds like?
                3. "d-o-v-e" sounds like?
                4. Quickly read the word aloud.

Blend "age" words = long "a" sound with an "e": page, sage, wage.

p***age***:   1. "a-g-e" sounds like?
                2. "p" sounds like?
                3. "p-a-g-e" sounds like?
                4. Quickly read the word aloud.

s***age***:   1. "a-g-e" sounds like?
                2. "s" sounds like?
                3. "s-a-g-e" sounds like?
                4. Quickly read the word aloud.

w***age***:   1. "a-g-e" sounds like?
                2. "w" sounds like?
                3. "w-a-g-e" sounds like?
                4. Quickly read the word aloud.

Blend "ate" = long "a" with silent "e" : date, plate, fate.

d*ate*:
1. "a-t-e" sounds like?
2. "d" sounds like?
3. "d-a-t-e" sounds like?
4. Quickly read the word aloud.

pl*ate*:
1. "a-t-e" sounds like?
2. "l" sounds like?
3. "p" sounds like?
4. "p-l-a-t-e" sounds like?
5. Quickly read the word aloud.

f*ate*:
1. "a-t-e" sounds like?
2. "f" sounds like?
3. "f-a-t-e" sounds like?
4. Quickly read the word aloud.

Blend "ast" = short "a" sound: fast, past, cast.

f*ast*:
1. "a-s-t" sounds like?
2. "f" sounds like?
3. "f-a-s-t" sounds like?
4. Quickly read the word aloud.

p*ast*:
1. "a-s-t" sounds like?
2. "p" sounds like?
3. "p-a-s-t" sounds like?
4. Quickly read the word aloud.

c*ast*:
1. "a-s-t" sounds like?
2. "c" sounds like?
3. "c-a-s-t" sounds like?
4. Quickly read the word aloud.

Blend "ane" = long "a" sound with silent "e": cane, lane, sane.

c***ane***:
    1. "a-n-e" sounds like?
    2. "c" sounds like?
    3. "c-a-n-e" sounds like?
    4. Quickly read the word aloud.

l***ane***:
    1. "a-n-e" sounds like?
    2. "l" sounds like?
    3. "l-a-n-e" sounds like?
    4. Quickly read the word aloud.

s***ane***:
    1. "a-n-e" sounds like?
    2. "s" sounds like?
    3. "s-a-n-e" sounds like?
    4. Quickly read the word aloud.

Blend "ell" words = short "e" sound: tell, bell, swell.

t***ell***:
    1. "l-l" sounds like?
    2. "e" sounds like?
    3. "t" sounds like?
    4. "t-e-l-l" sounds like?
    5. Quickly read the word aloud.

b***ell***:
    1. "l-l" sounds like?
    2. "e" sounds like?
    3. "b" sounds like?
    4. "b-e-l-l" sounds like?
    5. Quickly read the word aloud.

sw***e*ll**:   1. "l-l" sounds like?
         2. "e" sounds like?
         3. "w" sounds like?
         4. "s" sounds like?
         5. "s-w-e-l-l" sounds like?
         6. Quickly read the word aloud.

Blend "ill" words = short "i" sound: pill, silly, drill.

p***i*ll**:   1. "l-l" sounds like?
         2. "i" sounds like?
         3. "p" sounds like?
         4. "p-i-l-l" sounds like?
         5. Quickly read the word aloud.

s***ill***y: 1. "y" sounds like?
         2. "l-l" sounds like?
         3. "i" sounds like?
         4. "s" sounds like?
         5. "s-i-l-l-y" sounds like?
         6. Quickly read the word aloud.

dr***i*ll**:   1. "l-l" sounds like?
         2. "i" sounds like?
         3. "r" sounds like?
         4. "d" sounds like?
         5. "d-r-i-l-l" sounds like?
         6. Quickly read the word aloud.

Blends "ale" = long "a" sound with silent "e": pale, tale, sale.

p*ale*:
1. "a-l-e" sounds like?
2. "p" sounds like?
3. "p-a-l-e" sounds like?
4. Quickly read the word aloud.

t*ale*:
1. "a-l-e" sounds like?
2. "t" sounds like?
3. "t-a-l-e" sounds like?
4. Quickly read the word aloud.

s*ale*:
1. "a-l-e" sounds like?
2. "s" sounds like?
3. "s-a-l-e" sounds like?
4. Quickly read the word aloud.

Blend "oll" words = long "o" sound: dolly, jolly, collie.

d*oll*y:
1. "y" sounds like?
2. "o-l-l" sounds like?
3. "d" sounds like?
4. "d-o-l-l-y" sounds like?
5. Quickly read the words aloud.

j*oll*y:
1. "y" sounds like?
2. "o-l-l" sounds like?
3. "j" sounds like?
4. "j-o-l-l-y" sounds like?
5. Quickly read the word aloud.

c*oll*ie:
1. "e" sounds like?
2. "i" sounds like?
3. "o-l-l" sounds like?
4. "c" sounds like?
5. "c-o-l-l-i-e" sounds like?
6. Quickly read the word aloud.

Blend "oke" = long "o" sound with silent "e": token, joke.

t*oke*n:
1. "n" sounds like?
2. "o-k-e" sounds like?
3. "t" sounds like?
4. "t-o-k-e-n" sounds like?
5. Quickly read the word aloud.

j*oke*:
1. "o-k-e" sounds like?
2. "j" sounds like?
3. "j-o-k-e" sounds like?
4. Quickly read the word aloud.

Blend "if" = short "i" sound: rift, stiff, jiffy.

r*if*t:
1. "t" sounds like?
2. "i-f" sounds like?
3. "r" sounds like?
4. "r-i-f-t" sounds like?
5. Quickly read the word aloud.

st*if*f:
1. "f-f" sounds like?
2. "i" sounds like?
3. "t" sounds like?
4. "s" sounds like?
5. "s-t-i-f-f" sounds like?
6. Quickly read the word aloud.

j***if***fy:
1. "y" sounds like?
2. "f-f" sounds like?
3. "i" sounds like?
4. "j" sounds like?
5. "j-i-f-f-y" sounds like?
6. Quickly read the word aloud.

"ade" = long "a" sound with silent "e": made, trade, grade.

m***ade***:
1. "a-d-e" sounds like?
2. "m" sounds like?
3. "m-a-d-e" sounds like?
4. Quickly read the word aloud.

tr***ade***:
1. "a-d-e" sounds like?
2. "r" sounds like?
3. "t" sounds like?
4. "t-r-a-d-e" sounds like?
5. Quickly read the word aloud.

gr***ade***:
1. "a-d-e" sounds like?
2. "r" sounds like?
3. "g" sounds like?
4. "g-r-a-d-e" sounds like?
5. Quickly read the word aloud.

Blend "uff" = "uh" sound (schwa): cuff, stuff, puffy.

c<u>uff</u>:
1. "u-f-f" sounds like?
2. "c" sounds like?
3. "c-u-f-f" sounds like?
4. Quickly read the word aloud.

st<u>uff</u>:
1. "u-f-f" sounds like?
2. "t" sounds like?
3. "s" sounds like?
4. "s-t-u-f-f" sounds like?
5. Quickly read the word aloud.

p<u>uff</u>y:
1. "y" sounds like?
2. "u-f-f" sounds like?
3. "p" sounds like?
4. "p-u-f-f-y" sounds like?
5. Quickly read the word aloud.

Digraph "le" words: able, fable, table.

ab<u>le</u>:
1. "l-e" sounds like?
2. "b" sounds like?
3. "a" sounds like?
4. "a-b-l-e" sounds like?
5. Quickly read the word aloud.

fab**le**:   1. "l-e" sounds like?
                2. "b" sounds like?
                3. "a" sounds like?
                4. "f" sounds like?
                5. "f-a-b-l-e" sounds like?
                6. Quickly read the word aloud.

tab**le**:   1. "l-e" sounds like?
                2. "b" sounds like?
                3. "a" sounds like?
                4. "t" sounds like?
                5. "t-a-b-l-e" sounds make?
                6. Quickly read the word aloud.

Blend "ink" words = short "i" sound: mink, wink, think.

m*in*k: 1. "i-n-k" sounds like?
                2. "m" sounds like?
                3. "m-i-n-k" sounds like?
                4. Quickly read the word aloud.

w*in*k: 1. "i-n-k" sounds like?
                2. "w" sounds like?
                3. "w-i-n-k" sound like?
                4. Quickly read the word aloud.

th*in*k: 1. "i-n-k" sounds like?
                2. "t-h" sounds like?
                3. "t-h-i-n-k" sounds like?
                4. Quickly read the word aloud.
                5. What is another name for the "th" sound? **(digraph)**

Blend "ob" = short "o" sound: job, robin, mob.

j**ob**:
1. "o-b" sounds like?
2. "j" sounds like?
3. "j-o-b" sounds like?
4. Quickly read the word aloud.

r**ob**in:
1. "n" sounds like?
2. "i" sounds like?
3. "o-b" sounds like?
4. "r" sounds like?
5. "r-o-b-i-n" sounds like?
6. Quickly read the word aloud.

m**ob**:
1. "o-b" sounds like?
2. "m" sounds like?
3. "m-o-b" sounds like?
4. Quickly read the word aloud.

Blend "is" = short "i" sound: this, sister, mister

th*is*:
1. "i-s" sounds like?
3. "t-h" sounds like?
4. "t-h-i-s" sounds like?
5. Quickly read the word aloud.

s*is*ter:
1. "e-r" sounds like?
2. "t" sounds like?
3. "i-s" sounds like?
4. The first "s" sounds like?
5. "s-i-s-t-e-r" sounds like?
6. Quickly read the word aloud.

m*is*ter: 1. "e-r" sounds like?
              2. "t" sounds like?
              3. "i-s" sounds like?
              4. "m" sounds like?
              5. "m-i-s-t-e-r" sounds like?
              6. Quickly read the word aloud.

Blend "on" = short "o" vowel sound: honest, upon, pond.

h*on*est: 1. "s-t" sounds like?
              2. "e" sounds like?
              3. "o-n" sounds like?
              4. "h" sounds like?
              5. "h-o-n-e-s-t" sounds like?
              6. Quickly read the word aloud.

up*on*:   1. "o-n" sounds like?
              2. "p" sounds like?
              3. "u" sounds like?
              4. "u-p-o-n" sounds like?
              5. Quickly read the word aloud.

p*on*d: 1. "d" sounds like?
              2. "o-n" sounds like?
              3. "p" sounds like?
              4. "p-o-n-d" sounds like?
              5. Quickly read the word aloud.

Blend "ub" = short "u" sound: rub, snub, cub.

r*ub*:   1. "u-b" sounds like?
              2. "r" sounds like?
              3. "r-u-b" sounds like?
              4. Quickly read the word aloud.

sn**ub**: 1. "u-b" sounds like?
2. "n" sounds like?
3. "s" sounds like?
4. "s-n-u-b" sounds like?
5. Quickly read the word aloud.

c**ub**: 1. "u-b" sounds like?
2. "c" sounds like?
3. "c-u-b" sounds like?
4. Quickly read the word aloud.

Blend "ull" = short "u" sound: dull, sullen.

d**ull**: 1. "u-l-l" sounds like?
2. "d" sounds like?
3. "d-u-l-l" sounds like?
4. Quickly read the word aloud.

s**ull**en: 1. "n" sounds like?
2. "e" sounds like?
3. "u-l-l" sounds like?
4. "s" sounds like?
5. "s-u-l-l-e-n" sounds like?
6. Quickly read the word aloud.

Blend "ac" = short "a" sound: facts, actor, actress.

f**ac**ts: 1. "s" sounds like?
2. "t" sounds like?
3. "a-c" sounds like?
4. "f" sounds like?
5. "f-a-c-t-s" sounds like?
6. Quickly read the word aloud.

actor:
1. "o-r" sounds like?
2. "t" sounds like?
3. "a-c" sounds like?
4. "a-c-t-o-r" sounds like?
5. Quickly read the words aloud.

actress:
1. "s-s" sounds like?
2. "e" sounds like?
3. "r" sounds like?
4. "t" sounds like?
5. "a-c" sounds like?
6. "a-c-t-r-e-s-s" sounds like? Quickly read the word aloud.

Blend "af" = short "a" sound: raft, after, staff.

r**af**t:
1. "t" sounds like?
2. "a-f" sounds like?
3. "r" sounds like?
4. "r-a-f-t" sounds like?
5. Quickly read the word aloud.

after:
1. "e-r" sounds like?
2. "t" sounds like?
3. "a-f" sounds like?
4. "a-f-t-e-r" sounds like?
5. Quickly read the word aloud.
6. What is another name for letters "e-r"? **(blend)**

st**aff**:
1. "a-f-f" sounds like?
2. "t" sounds like?
3. "s" sounds like?
4. "s-t-a-f-f" sounds like?
5. Quickly read the word aloud.

Blend "od" = short "o" sound: rod, trod

r**od**:
1. "o-d" sounds like?
2. "r" sounds like?
3. "r-o-d" sounds like?
4. Quickly read the word aloud.

tr**od**:
1. "o-d" sounds like?
2. "r" sounds like?
3. "t" sounds like?
4. "t-r-o-d" sounds like?
5. Quickly read the word aloud.

Combination "tion" = "shun" sound: action, fraction, motion.

ac**tion**:
1. "t-i-o-n" sounds like?
2. "c" sounds like?
3. "a" sounds like?
4. "a-c-t-i-o-n" sounds like?
5. Quickly read the word aloud.

frac**tion**:
1. "t-i-o-n" sounds like?
2. "c" sounds like?
3. "a" sounds like?
4. "r" sounds like?
5. "f" sounds like?
6. "f-r-a-c-t-i-o-n" sounds like?
7. Quickly read the word aloud.

mo**tion**:
1. "t-i-o-n" sounds like?
2. "o" sounds like?
3. "m" sounds like?
4. "m-o-t-i-o-n" sounds like?
5. Quickly read the word aloud.

Blend "ig" words = short "i" sound: jig, pig, sprig.

j*ig*:
1. "i-g" sounds like?
2. "j" sounds like?
3. "j-i-g" sounds like?
4. Quickly read the word aloud.

p*ig*:
1. "i-g" sounds like?
2. "p" sounds like?
3. "p-i-g" sounds like?
4. Quickly read the word aloud.

spr*ig*:
1. "i-g" sounds like?
3. "r" sounds like?
4. "p" sounds like?
5. "s" sounds like?
6. "s-p-r-i-g" sounds like?
7. Quickly read the word aloud.
8. What is another name for letters "s-p"? **(blend)**

Blend "ip" words = short "i" sound: dip, chip, flip.

d*ip*:
1. "i-p" sounds like?
2. "d" sounds like?
3. "d-i-p" sounds like?
4. Quickly read the word aloud.

ch*ip*:
1. "i-p" sounds like?
2. "c-h" sounds like?
3. "c-h-i-p" sounds like?
4. Quickly read the word aloud.
5. What is another name for letters "c-h"? **(diagraph)**

fl*ip*:
1. "i-p" sounds like?
2. "f-l" sounds like?
3. "f-l-i-p" sounds like?
4. Quickly read the word aloud.
5. What is another name for letters "f-l"? **(blend)**

Blend "ug" = short "u" sound: bug, rug, snug.

b*ug*:
1. "u-g" sounds like?
2. "b" sounds like?
3. "b-u-g" sounds like?
4. Quickly read the word aloud.

r*ug*:
1. "u-g" sounds like?
2. "r" sounds like?
3. "r-u-g" sounds like?
4. Quickly read the word aloud.

sn*ug*:
1. "u-g" sounds like?
2. "n" sounds like?
3. "s" sounds like?
4. "s-n-u-g" sounds like?
5. Quickly read the word aloud.

Blend "id" = short "i" sound: did, slid, hidden.

d*id*:
1. "i-d" sounds like?
2. "d" sounds like?
3. "d-i-d" sounds like?
4. Quickly read the word aloud.

sl*id*: 1. "i-d" sounds like?
       2. "l" sounds like?
       3. "s" sounds like?
       4. "s-l-i-d" sounds like?
       5. Quickly read the word aloud.

h*id*den: 1. "n" sounds like?
       2. "e" sounds like?
       3. "d" sounds like?
       4. "i-d" sounds like?
       5. "h" sounds like?
       6. "h-i-d-d-e-n" sounds like?
       7. Quickly read the word aloud.

Blend "en" = short "e" sound: ten, end, men

t*en*: 1. "e-n" sounds like?
       2. "t" sounds like?
       3. "t-e-n" sounds like?
       4. Quickly read the word aloud.

*en*d: 1. "d" sounds like?
       2. "e-n" sounds like?
       3. "e-n-d" sounds like?
       4. Quickly read the word aloud.

m*en*: 1. "e-n" sounds like?
       2. "m" sounds like?
       3. "m-e-n" sounds like?
       4. Quickly read the word aloud.

Digraph "ed" = ending "t" sound: stopped, helped

stopp**ed**: 1. "e-d" sounds like?
            2. "p-p" sounds like?
            3. "o" sounds like?
            4. "s-t" sounds like?
            5. "s-t-o-p-p-e-d" sounds like?
            6. Quickly read the word aloud.
            7. What is the other name for "e-d"? **(blend & digraph)**

help**ed**: 1. "e-d" sounds like?
            2. "p" sounds like?
            3. "l" sounds like?
            4. "e" sounds like?
            5. "h" sounds like?
            6. "h-e-l-p-e-d" sounds like?
            7. Quickly read the word aloud.

.

Blend "ed" words= Short "e" sound: wanted, started, decided.

want*ed*: 1. "e-d" sounds like?
            2. "t" sounds like?
            3. "n" sounds like?
            4. "a" sounds like?
            5. "w" sounds like?
            6. "w-a-n-t-e-d" sounds like?
            7. Quickly read the word aloud.

start*ed*:
1. "e-d" sounds like?
2. "t" sounds like?
3. "r" sounds like?
4. "a" sounds like?
5. "s-t" sounds like?
6. "s-t-a-r-t-e-d" sounds like?
7. Quickly read the word aloud.
8. What is another name for "s-t"? (**blend**)

decid*ed*:
1. "e-d" sounds like?
2. Second "d" sounds like?
3. "i" sounds like?
4. "c" sounds like? (**S sound**)
5. "e" sounds like?
6. First "d" sounds like?
7. "d-e-c-i-d-e-d" sounds like?
8. Quickly read the word aloud.

Blend "ud" = short "u" sound: bud, puddle, mud.

b***ud***:
1. "u-d" sounds like?
2. "b" sounds like?
3. "b-u-d" sounds like?
4. Quickly read the word aloud.

p***ud***dle:
1. "l-e" sounds like?
2. "d" sounds like?
3. "u-d" sounds like?
4. "p" sounds like?
5. "p-u-d-d-l-e" sounds like?
6. Quickly read the word aloud.

m**ud**:   1. "u-d" sounds like?
          2. "m" sounds like?
          3. "m-u-d" sounds like?
          4. Quickly read the word aloud.

Blend "ut" = short "u" sound: nut, shut, cut.

n**ut**:   1. "u-t" sounds like?
          2. "n" sounds like?
          3. "n-u-t" sounds like?
          4. Quickly read the word aloud?

sh**ut**: 1. "u-t" sounds like?
          2. "s-h" sounds like?
          3. "s-h-u-t" sounds like?
          4. Quickly read the word aloud.

c**ut**:   1. "u-t" sounds like?
          2. "c" sounds like?
          3. "c-u-t" sounds like?
          4. Quickly read the word aloud.

Blend "em" words= Short "e" sound: gem, empty, them.

g**em**:   1. "e-m" sounds like?
          2. "g" sounds like?
          3. "g-e-m" sounds like?
          4. Quickly read the word aloud.

empty: 1. "y" sounds like?
          2. "t" sounds like?
          3. "p" sounds like?
          4. "e-m" sounds like?
          5. "e-m-p-t-y" sounds like?
          6. Quickly read the word aloud.

th***em***:   1. "e-m" sounds like?
                2. "t-h" sounds like?
                3. "t-h-e-m" sounds like?
                4. Quickly read the word aloud.

Combination "ent" words: lent, cent, rent

l**ent**:   1. "e-n-t" sounds like?
             2. "l" sounds like?
             3. "l-e-n-t" sounds like?
             4. Quickly read the word aloud.

c**ent**:   1. "e-n-t" sounds like?
             2. "c" sounds like?
             3. "c-e-n-t" sound like?
             4. Quickly read the word aloud.

r**ent**:   1. "e-n-t" sounds like?
             2. "r" sounds like?
             3. "r-e-n-t" sounds like?
             4. Quickly read the word aloud.

Combination "ake"= Long "a" and Silent "e" words: bake, take, make.

b***ake***:   1. "a-k-e" sounds like?
             2. "b" sounds like?
             3. "b-a-k-e sounds like?
             4.Quickly read the word aloud.

t*ake*:   1. "a-k-e" sounds like?
            2. "t" sounds like?
            3. "t-a-k-e" sounds like?
            4. Quickly read the word aloud.

m*ake*:   1. "a-k-e" sounds like?
            2. "m" sounds like?
            3. "m-a-k-e" sounds like?
            4. Quickly read the word aloud.

Combination "ide" = Long "i" and Silent "e" words: tide, ride, slide.

t*ide*:   1. "i-d-e" sounds like?
            2. "t" sounds like?
            3. "t-i-d-e" sounds like?
            4. Quickly read the word aloud.
            5. What's the rule with silent "e"? **(Make vowel say its name)**

r*ide*:   1. "i-d-e" sounds like?
            2. "r" sounds like?
            3. "r-i-d-e" sounds like?
            4. Quickly read the words aloud.

sl*ide*:   1. "i-d-e" sounds like?
            2. "l" sounds like?
            3. "s" sounds like?
            4. "s-l-i-d-e" sounds like?
            5. Quickly read the word aloud.
            6. Another name for letters "s-l" **(blend)**

Blend "up" = short "u" sound: pup, upset, cup.

p***up***:
1. "u-p" sounds like?
2. "p" sounds like?
3. "p-u-p" sounds like?
4. Quickly read the word aloud.

upset:
1. "t" sounds like?
2. "e" sounds like?
3. "s" sounds like?
4. "u-p" sounds like?
5. "u-p-s-e-t" sounds like?
6. Quickly read the word aloud.

c***up***:
1. "u-p" sounds like?
2. "c" sounds like?
3. "c-u-p" sound makes?
4. Quickly read the word aloud.
5. Another name for letters "u-p" **(blend)**

Combination "est" = short "e" sound: best, test, nest.

b***est***:
1. "e-s-t" sounds like?
2. "b" sounds like?
3. "b-e-s-t" sounds like?
4. Quickly read the word aloud.

t**est**:	1. "e-s-t" sounds like?
    2. "t" sounds like?
    3. "t-e-s-t" sounds like?
    4. Quickly read the word aloud

n**est**:	1. "e-s-t" sounds like?
    2. "n" sounds like?
    3. "n-e-s-t" sounds like?
    4. Quickly read the word aloud.

Combination "ied" = long "i" sound: lied, tried, cried.

l**ied**:	1. "i-e-d" sounds like?
    2. "l" sounds like?
    3. "l-i-e-d" sounds like?
    4. Quickly read the word aloud.
    5. Another name for letters "i-e"? **(diphthong)**

t**ied**:	1. "i-e-d" sounds like?
    2. "t" sounds like?
    3. "t-i-e-d" sounds like?
    4. Quickly read the word aloud.

cr**ied**:	1. "i-e-d" sounds like?
    2. "r" sounds like?
    3. "c" sounds like?
    4. "c-r-i-e-d" sounds like?
    5. Quickly read the word aloud.

Blend "al" = short "a" sound: p*a*l, r*a*lly, can*a*l.

p*al*:
1. "a-l" sounds like?
2. "p" sounds like?
3. "p-a-l" sounds like?
4. Quickly read the word aloud.

r*al*ly:
1. "y" sounds like?
2. "l" sounds like?
3. "a-l" sounds like?
4. "r" sounds like?
5. "r-a-l-l-y" sounds like?
6. Quickly read the word aloud.

can*al*:
1. "a-l" sounds like?
2. "n" sounds like?
3. "a" sounds like?
4. "c" sounds like?
5. "c-a-n-a-l" sounds like?
6. Quickly read the word aloud.

Blend "ape" = long "a" sound with silent "e" words: cape, shape.

c*ape*:
1. "a-p-e" sounds like?
2. "c" sounds like?
3. "c-a-p-e" sounds like?
4. Quickly read the word aloud.

sh*a*pe: 1. "a-p-e" sounds like?
2. "s-h" sounds like?
3. "s-h-a-p-e" sounds like?
4. Quickly read the word aloud.

Digraph "oa" = long "o" sound: oats, coat, loan.

*oa*ts: 1. "s" sounds like?
2. "t" sounds like?
3. "o-a" sounds like?
4. "o-a-t-s" sounds like?
5. Quickly read the word aloud.
6. What is the rule on two vowels together? **(First vowels says sound)**

c*oa*t: 1. "t" sounds like?
2. "o-a" sounds like?
3. "c" sounds like?
4. "c-o-a-t" sounds like?
5. Quickly read the word aloud.

l*oa*n: 1. "n" sounds like?
2. "o-a" sounds like?
3. "l" sounds like?
4. "l-o-a-n" sounds like?
5. Quickly read the word aloud.

Combination "ock" = short "o" sound: dock, stock, rock.

d**ock**:
1. "o-c-k" sounds like?
2. "d" sounds like?
3. "d-o-c-k" sounds like?
4. Quickly read the word aloud.

st**ock**:
1. "o-c-k" sounds like?
2. "s-t" sounds like?
3. "s-t-o-c-k" sounds like?
4. Quickly read the word aloud.

r**ock**:
1. "o-c-k" sounds like?
2. "r" sounds like?
3. "r-o-c-k" sounds like?
4. Quickly read the word aloud.

Combination "ire" = long "i" sound with silent "e": hire, fire, wire.

h**ire**:
1. "i-r-e" sounds like?
2. "h" sounds like?
3. "h-i-r-e" sounds like?
4. Quickly read the word aloud?

f**ire**:
1. "i-r-e" sounds like?
2. "f" sounds like?
3. "f-i-r-e" sounds like?
4. Quickly read the word aloud.

w*ire*:
1. "i-r-e" sounds like?
2. "w" sounds like?
3. "w-i-r-e" sounds like?
4. Quickly read the word aloud.

Digraph "ue" = "oo" sound (open sound): due, glue, true.

d<u>ue</u>:
1. "u-e" sounds like?
2. "d" sounds like?
3. "d-u-e" sounds like?
4. Quickly read the word aloud.

gl<u>ue</u>:
1. "u-e" sounds like?
2. "l" sounds like?
3. "g" sounds like?
4. "g-l-u-e" sounds like?
5. Quickly read the word aloud.

tr<u>ue</u>:
1. "u-e" sounds like?
2. "r" sounds like?
3. "t" sounds like?
4. "t-r-u-e" sounds like?
5. Quickly read the word aloud.

Digraph "ur" words: fur, turn, curb.

f<u>ur</u>:
1. "u-r" sounds like?
2. "f" sounds like?
3. "f-u-r" sounds like?
4. Quickly read the word aloud.

t<u>ur</u>n: 1. "n" sounds like?
        2. "u-r" sounds like?
        3. "t" sounds like?
        4. "t-u-r-n" sounds like?
        5. Quickly read the word aloud.

c<u>ur</u>b: 1. "b" sounds like?
        2. "u-r" sounds like?
        3. "c" sounds like?
        4. "c-u-r-b" sounds like?
        5. Quickly read the word aloud.

Blend "ir" words: stir, first, bird.

st<u>ir</u>: 1. "i-r" sounds like?
        2. "s-t" sounds like?
        3. "s-t-i-r" sounds like?
        4. Quickly read the word aloud.
        5. What is another name for "i-r"? **(diphthong)**

f<u>ir</u>st: 1. "s-t" sounds like?
        2. "i-r" sounds like?
        3. "f" sounds like?
        4. "f-i-r-s-t" sounds like?
        5. Quickly read the word aloud.

b<u>ir</u>d: 1. "d" sounds like?
        2. "i-r" sounds like?
        3. "b" sounds like?
        4. "b-i-r-d" sounds like?
        5. Quickly read the word aloud.

Combination "ure" words = short "u" sound with silent "e": sure, pure, cure.

s**ure**:
    1. "u-r-e" sounds like?
    2. "s" sounds like?
    3. "s-u-r-e" sounds like?
    4. Quickly read the word aloud.

p**ure**:
    1. "u-r-e" sounds like?
    2. "p" sounds like?
    3. "p-u-r-e" sounds like?
    4. Quickly read the word aloud.

c**ure**:
    1. "u-r-e" sounds like?
    2. "c" sounds like?
    3. "c-u-r-e" sounds like?
    4. Quickly read the word aloud.

Combination "air" words: pair, fairy, dairy.

p**air**:
    1. "a-i-r" sounds like?
    2. "p" sounds like?
    3. "p-a-i-r" sounds like?
    4. Quickly read the word aloud.

f**air**y:
    1. "y" sounds like?
    2. "a-i-r" sounds like?
    3. "f" sounds like?
    4. "f-a-i-r-y" sounds like?
    5. Quickly read the word aloud.

d**air**y"   1. "y" sounds like?
2. "a-i-r" sounds like?
3. "d" sounds like?
4. "d-a-i-r-y" sounds like?
5. Quickly read the word aloud.

The next section is a compilation of short stories utilizing the the different vowel sounds as well as different blends and digraphs. It is my hope to give you examples of sentence building ideas that you can do with your students or children to build knowledge as well as have fun with learning. I fully believe getting students engaged in their learning will promote growth in all academic areas. After you will find other resources in further educating your students in the skills needed to read and eventually write about what they read. Comprehension is a vital part of reading. I focus a whole section on how to help further students' skills in these areas as well. Lastly, I provide a list of books students will need to read in the older years, which can also assist in their progression as youths.

Short Stories

Short "a" Vowel:

Puffy <u>ran</u> to meet Fluffy the cat in the park. A <u>man</u> set a <u>pan</u> of milk down for them to eat. Both Puffy and Fluffy saw a <u>bat</u> flying. Before Puffy and Fluffy could catch the <u>bat</u>, the <u>bat</u> flew away.

Long "a" Vowel:

(Bread is an irregularity because it does not follow the rule). Two vowels together makes the first vowel long.

Buffy, <u>wakes</u> up and <u>loosk</u> at the <u>snake</u>. Wide <u>awake</u>, Buffy <u>chased</u> and <u>played</u> with the <u>snake</u>. The <u>snake</u> made his way into a hole. Buffy gave up playing with the <u>snake</u>. Buffy went into the <u>bakery</u> hoping to find some bread at the <u>bakery</u>. Buffy <u>ate</u> <u>bakery</u> bread until he was full.

Schwa "a" words:

We are going to eat a <u>salad</u> for lunch. You can have a small <u>salad</u> or big <u>salad</u>. On the shelf <u>above</u>, desserts can be seen. They are cream puffs and <u>banana</u> cupcakes. Some cupcakes look like <u>zebras</u>.

"ar" with an "air" sound:

"Will you please <u>carry</u> a bag for me?" asked <u>Larry</u>. Please take <u>care</u> not to drop it. Take <u>careful</u> <u>care</u> of my outfit. I could not <u>bare</u> it if you should <u>dare</u> to drop it in the puddle of water. In my bag is my wedding dress to <u>marry</u> <u>Harry</u>.

The letters "ar" = "r" sound too:

Please don't <u>dart</u> across the street, Dan. You must always look both ways before <u>starting</u> across the street. A <u>car</u> could hit you and send you <u>far</u> into the sky. You might feel like you were sent to <u>mars</u>. Dan, by touching the <u>bar</u>, the light will turn green, and we will walk across the street. The light works in the <u>dark</u> too.

Short "e" Vowel:

"Bet you can't fly like a bird," said Mark. "Well, no one can fly like a bird," remarked Tom. Set everything on the bench. "I will stand on the bench," said Mark. "Get my wings and I will flap my wings like a bird and land on the sand like a bird," said Mark.

Long "e" Vowel:

Tom loves to eat meat and he likes to eat beans with his meat. After eating meat, Tom likes to eat a dish of ice cream. Before bed, Tom loves to eat two bags of peanuts with his ice cream.

Short "i" Vowel:

Sally and Mary went for a walk in the woods. It happened on a cold nippy night. A shrill sound came from the trees. Both girls froze in their tracks. Then they hid behind some bushes. A light came on and the girls were happy because they didn't step into a deep dark pit.

Long "i" Vowel:

"Please get me some ice for my drink," asked Mike. "Okay, said Sam, only if you get me some ice cream." "I love icy ice cream." "Me too," said Mike. Mike replied, "Let us slide down the big slide." Sam jumped off the diving board and into the pool. Mike said, "Watch me glide down the slide and into the pool too."

Short "o" Vowel:

"Did you see the mop?" asked Bill. No, I was too busy watching someone try to rob my pop. A cop or policeman stopped the robber at the stop sign. The robber was arrested.

Long "o" Vowel:

"Will you please open the door for me?" asked Joe. My hands are full of polls for ice skating. "Alright," said Bob, but first we need to go over to Sam's house. "Why Sam's house?" asked Joe. "So, we can go ice skating together," remarked Bob.

Open "oo" Vowel:

"Jay took my book at <u>noon</u>," remarked Joy. I'm sure he will return my book very <u>soon</u>. I hope Jay will put my book back in the nook. Jay is not a <u>fool.</u> Joy, I know he acts <u>too</u> <u>cool</u> and <u>goofy</u> about my <u>cartoon</u> books that I gave him to read. I'm sure he'll return your book, to your <u>nook.</u>

"We will fly to the <u>moon soon.</u>" said Fran. I will bet you my <u>spoon</u> over it. We will eat tubes of <u>food</u> on the trip. "I hope to see the <u>moon</u> and stars twinkle <u>soon</u>." said Sky.

Short "u" Vowel:

"Let the dust settle before we trim the <u>bushes</u>." said Roy. The <u>sun</u> will heat up the sky, and we must finish trimming the <u>bushes</u>. After trimming the <u>bushes</u>, we can eat hot dogs on a <u>bun</u>. "We must hurry before the hot dog <u>buns</u> are eaten by others," said Bob. Thank goodness we are done. We will have to <u>run</u> to get in line for our hot dog <u>bun</u>.

"Have you seen my chewing <u>gum</u>?" asked, Joe. I must catch the <u>bus</u> and I want to take my <u>gum</u> to share with other guys playing baseball. It was near my coffee <u>mug</u>. No, I didn't see it. Your friend named <u>Bud</u> might have taken the pack when he caught the <u>bus</u>. He didn't get a ride in his Dad's <u>truck</u>? His Dad's <u>truck</u> was too <u>muddy</u> to drive and needed to be washed.

Long "u" Vowel:

<u>Music</u> makes most people feel happy. Some people want to dance to the music. In the springtime, a <u>tuba</u> gives a full sound to the band <u>music</u>. Our small musical band will ride in a wagon that is pulled by a <u>mule</u>. We will make jubilant <u>music</u> for everyone to hear.

A band uniform is <u>cute</u> but too hot to wear on a warm day in a parade. Music can <u>amuse</u> a person in a <u>huge</u> crowd of people. The on lookers who watch the parade should have a large glass ice <u>cubes</u> in a cold drink that they can drink.

Rocket Reader 1 ---- Sight Words

Place on index cards for student to quickly read aloud the word they are shown. Most of the words are written in different genre writings.

the	he	first	both	work	water
a	under	get	of	for	put
and	it	now	never	here	think
to	with	our	same	day	took
as	even	another	does	night	in
on	after	last	left	called	they
at	before	great	until	look	her
I	there	cane	almost	next	all
all	this	we	right	hand	days
two	had	him	used	far	let
may	not	when	take	head	room
then	are	who	three	yet	want
do	but	will	use	better	done
my	from	no	again	set	open
mine	have	if	place	told	white
us	or	out	over	nothing	kind
old	which	so	men	car	different
off	were	said	me	why	door
come	would	what	did	didn't	whole
go	their	up	back	eyes	above
house	been	it	your	find	hands
big	has	into	just	knew	show
four	more	them	people	city	five

miss	about	can	Mr.	give	gave
today	play	new	how	face	feet
children	only	some	too	home	across
help	other	time	little	went	seen
it's	could	each	good	say	really
name	help	those	very	school	together
that	first	still	make	don't	money
is	any	own	see	away	sure
was	these	long	moose	real	some
real	letter	egg	shoe	home	drink
having	art	pig	bread	yellow	blue
car	leave	seven	window	floor	bus
I'm	plan	air	road	sister	blew
tell	sound	sister	making	gone	full
car	leave	seven	floor	keep	believe
street	says	robin	early	brought	women
boy	man	around	need	charge	started
love	table	small	saw	board	cut
girl	must	found	best	west	down
six	years	Mrs.	church	east	point
mother	where	thought	light	high	between
run	much	part	thing	American	hurry
top	way	high	world	dog	present
bear	well	every	hear	company	should
doll	group	moon	heard	soon	red
through	horse	whose	night	aunt	book
ever	must	of	off	black	pink

slow	enough	lunch	animal	other	brown
seem	dress	able	balloon	cake	picture
close	already	name	pocket	found	turn
nose	next	nose	eye	worm	states
mine	sand	birthday	run	can	want
wanted	calf	hip	ten	green	orange
up	white	me	feet	weep	ask
short	funny	win	town	night	day
water	chilly	snow	cold	frozen	where

Comprehension is a Learned Skill.

Rules for staying focused in reading is easy to follow.

1. Read the title of the story. Next, make a *prediction* about the title of the story *before* reading it.

2. *Predict* what the *first* paragraph is about before reading it. Who are the *characters* in the story? Are they friends or enemies? Could a character be jealous, resentful, loving, or caring, humorous, obnoxious, competitive, or silly.

3. An *exposition* gives a description of the characters, personalities, the in the story or surrounding of where they are located. The *theme* is introduced by circumstances that take place in the exposition.

4. *Predict* the *second* paragraph before reading it and each of the following paragraphs before reading begins.

5. By gathering information as you read, make a prediction about the ending of the story.

6. Does the character have a title? (Dr., Mr., Mrs., Miss, Ms.) Your question will begin with "who". Who is Miss Taylor or Who is Dr. Sam? (Dentist or M.D.)

7. The setting in a story takes place at a (beach, river, stream, brook, lake, ranch, city, desert, jungle, mountains, a canyon, cottage, farm, suburbs).

8. The time of year the story takes place in (spring, summer, autumn, winter).

9. Illustrations may give the time of year and the setting.

10. If a story is about a place or animal, your question will begin with "what."

Descriptive Stories

1. Is the character tall, short, muscular, stout, or slender?

2. Is the character young, teenager, middle age or a senior?

3. Color of hair, eyes, mustache, beard, short hair, medium length, long hair, or bald.

4. Visible scars or tattoos?

5. Collect as much physical detail about a character that one can in order to interpret the characters' purpose, behaviors, and more.

Narrative Stories

1. *Main character* of a story may have *internal conflict*. A character may have a fear of height or riding in an elevator. The main character will try to solve the problem in the story.

2. A *dynamic character* goes through changes in their *personality* and *attitude*. Shopping became a hardship in supplying June's family with enough food on the table to eat for dinner. A personality and attitude change occurred when June won a lottery ticket for twenty million dollars.

3. A *minor character* may be jealous or envious of the main character. An *external conflict* happens when the minor character tries to destroy the the reputation of a major character.

4. *Emotional feeling* uses expressive language. For instance, the character may exhibit a feeling of being cold, warm, frigid, happy or melancholy by the choice of words written.

5. *Dialogue* happens when two or more people meet in a story. In testing, they may ask for the *main point* of the conversation and *who is speaking*.

What are the four points of a Narrative?

1. A narrative has four points to a story. First, it has a *rising action* that is suspenseful.
    (A heavy set dark clothed person wearing a hoodie, gloves, and a pair of large muddy boots entered the college dean's office with a knife.)

2. The second strategy of a story must have a *climax.* A climax has tension and excitement.
    (The dean reached for his keys in his pocket. He heard a noise and reached for his gun instead. He threw open the office door.).

3. ***Falling Action*** occurs when the tension and excitement in the story is reduced.

   (Confronting the intruder with his gun, the hooded man dropped his knife to the floor. The intruder confessed he wanted a higher grade than the dean was giving him.).

4. In the last phase of a story, a story is *resolved*. Little details of the story are exposed and wrapped up before the ending. A ***resolution*** wraps up a story gathering loose ends together showing a decision was made.

   (Campus police arrived and the intruder received probation. He wouldn't be able to play sports again.).

Literary Terms

Hyperbole: Creates humor by over exaggeration. The exaggeration is not to be taken literally.
   A. I've been waiting ages for the bus.
   B. Your purse weighs a ton.

Metaphor: Comparing two things that are not alike such as people, places objects or animals. In a metaphor, the words *like* or *as* is <u>**never**</u> used to compare.
   A. Time flies.
   B. She has a bubbly personality.

Personification: By giving human qualities to a non-human being.
   A. My dog argued over the piece of meat.
   B. My alley cat snuggled his way into my lap.

Simile: A simile will compare two things that are different by using the words "like" or "as."
   A. He is busy **as** a bee and doesn't have time for me.

Idioms: Words describing a noun using feelings, speech, or action.
  A. That steak cost an arm and leg. (very costly).
  B. The ball is in his court. (a decision to be made).
  C. He blew his stack. (got angry).

Allusion: Compares a well—known story, an object or person.
  A. Bible story
  B. History
  C. Literature
    1. He was born with a silver spoon in his mouth.
    2. After a meal, our boss became a scrooge when it came to tipping a waiter.

Irony: Irony will ridicule, use humor or sarcasm.
  A. It took the locksmith forever to unlock the door.
  B. It is raining. Someone says, it is nice weather today.

Alliteration: A musical quality in the choice of words that are emphasized.
  A. **B**ecky's **b**eagle **b**arked and **b**ayed **b**ecoming **b**othersome for **B**illy.

Myth: A myth tries to explain the universe using gods and heroes. Someone made up or imaginary.
  A. Zeus was known to be the god of lightning and father to all minor gods and goddesses.

Characterization is developed by a character. A character's words and actions tell the story about him. The thoughts of a character may be told in the story. Opinions of others about a main character, minor or dynamic character may be told by describing the appearance of a character.

A **fact** can be proven.
  A. Abraham Lincoln was born on February 12th and George Washington was born on February 22nd.

Onomatopoeia will have words and sounds to imitate a noise.
    A. The bees **buzzed** around my head. (Describing a noun through words.)
    B. You could smell and hear the bacon **sizzle** in the frying pan.

Folklore is a story that has been passed down from generation to generation. Each culture has a legend, myth, folktale or fable.

Opinion happens when a person expresses a belief. An opinion cannot be proven.
    A. Strawberry ice cream is the best ice cream in the whole wide world.
    B. Ice helps make a drink taste better.

A **Fable** teaches a lesson about human nature through animals. The animals acts and speaks like a human being. A fable teaches a lesson.

A **Legend** is a popular historical story that had no verification. A legend may be about a famous personality who excels in a specific field or career.

Figures of Speech have many figures of speech to learn. They are anaphora, antimetabole, antithesis, apostrophe, assonance, metonymy, paradox, pun, synecdoche and understatement, oxymoron, and sardonic.

A **Flashback** is used to present a scene that took place in the past. The actress had an accident that caused amnesia. The actress had a flashback at what had occurred before the accident.

An **Act** is where a character has the chief role in a play. If an act is split into a smaller section, then it is called a scene.

Teleplay may become a television program or remain a live drama. On the floor spots are marked for the actor to stop and turn. Camera angles are addressed in directions for close up and for distance.

Autobiography is where an author writes about themselves.

Biography is about a politician, celebrity, or famous sports person.

In a **Narrative,** how does a character react to emotional words? Panic, fear, anger, gentleness, jealousy, friendship, withdrawn, bubbly, reticent, laid back, open, hostile etc.

Many areas of reading are tested and as a student, they must have knowledge in each area.

Literature	*Narrative*	*Directions*	*Sequencing*
Poems	*Science*	*History*	*Dialogue*
Drama	*Ballet*	*Opera*	*Myth*
Fable	*Compare and Contrast*		

History is interesting because you must know the leaders who fought for freedom and men who fought for dictatorship. Be ready to describe the commanders and the decisions they made and why they made the decision. Was it a good decision or an error in judgement? **Who, what happened, where (place).** Below one through four delve deeper to analyze a matter.

1. What event or issue happened that caused a leader to be concerned?

2. How did the event take place?

3. How did the issue get resolved?

There are several different purposes in writing to acknowledge.

    1. **A Narrative** tells a <u>story</u>.

    2. **Expository** writing <u>explains</u> and gives information.

    3. **Descriptive** <u>picture</u> in words of a place, someone, or an object. (a vase).

4. **Explanatory** writing gives <u>data</u>. It may concern a merger of a company and how it will affect the investors in the company.
    a. sales
    b. failing to meet expect quotas. (charts, graphs, percentages).

5. **Expressive** writing giving a person's <u>thoughts</u> and <u>emotions</u>.

6. **Persuasive** writing by attempting with words to <u>sway your opinion</u> to buy a product or vote for a specific candidate.

7. **Analytical** writing <u>exams material</u> presented.

The parent or friend must read the material prior to helping a person learn the steps to becoming a successful reader. No answers have been provided. Predicting the information given in each paragraph is necessary. Remember to make predictions about the title before each paragraph is read.

Do not read more than one story a night.

    Science and history reading takes patience because it is filled with information on events. The light bulb invention inspired the future to be a brighter place to live.

    History takes in emotional issues that crowd the scene. A right or wrong decision may be made at the time. How did the decision affect the future?

    Always ask how did the event take place?
    How did the issue get resolved?
    Why did the event or issue happen?

The following pages are examples of written works in various academic areas. Also provided are questions to ask about each writing. These are to give you examples of appropriate styles, concepts, and questions for you to work on with your students when working on both reading and writing.

Work Examples

General George Patton

George Patton made history with his armored tank division in World War I. In 1941, he trained the first and second armored division on the desert in Indio, California. By training on the desert, it helped Patton to get through Kasserine Pass in his advance through Tunisia in North Africa and all French Morocco. The first fighting Americans retreated 50 mile leaving tanks and armored vehicles.

By July 10, 1941, Patton was in charge of the seventh division which captured Sicily, Italy within thirty-eight days. Sicilians were happy.

In 1944, his tanks went ashore in Normandy, France. Patton worked under the direction of Dwight D. Eisenhower. Patton invaded German defenses and swept across France. By August 15, 1944, his men broke through the German lines by February 5, controlling several towns. He and his men managed to take the heart of Germany in the Battle of the Bulge. Advancing forward, he began his invasion on March 26th and continued his advance into Austria before the war ended.

Patton's aggressive and rapid style of taking swift action against the enemy and his knowledge of tanks gave him the upper hand in the war.

Who is the article about?

What was he in charge of in the military?

Where did he train in 1941?

Name one place in California that helped Patton to conquer Kasserine Pass and the German Army Fighting Force?

How did the training help him?

What equipment helped Patton defeat the Germans?

Where did the seventh division free an occupied territory?

How many days did it take Patton and his men to conquer a Sicilian Island?

Who was Patton's commander?

In 1944, Patton landed his men and tanks in which country?

Name the battle Patton fought and overtook the heart of German rule.

Before the war ended, what country did Patton give freedom to?

Vladimir Ilyich Ulyanov

I became a lawyer and I worked for the government in Russia. No one would have believed that I was a Russian Revolutionary rebel. In order to protect my family from the Tsar's, I shortened my name to Lenin in case I was arrested and put in jail. I went to meetings where Karl Marx and Friedrich Engels ideology was taught.

I wanted to make a change for the betterment of the Russian people. In the beginning there were a handful of us who stuck together. We had a dream to remove the Tsar family. We wondered how we could do it since none of us had a lot of money. Joseph Stalin and I became good friends. Stalin robbed several banks and was never caught. He supplied us with an abundance of cash so we could topple the Tsars.

We decided on a name, and we called our gang the Bolsheviks. Our plan was to put an end to the autocracy of the Tsars. We sold the idea that we could take possession of all their property and place them under the state control. In this way, everyone would have a job, but they would work for the government and not for themselves. People liked to eat and I made food scarce for the Russian people. Starvation took place and the people did not realize it was a manufactured scarcity.

We gained control of the oil and gas in Russia. We would decide how much oil would be produced. It gave us complete control of Russia. We were lucky the White leaders in the White Army were at odds with one another. Their morale was down and three White leaders in the White Army did not unite to fight us. They tried out doing one another and caused friction, losing sight of the goal to keep the Tsars and themselves safe. Otherwise, the Tsars would have remained in power.

I ruled Russia from 1917 to 1924. Many of our opponents were Eliminated just like the Tsars. Once in power, we changed our name from Bolsheviks to the Communist Party. I moved to Switzerland to live.

Joseph Stalin became the leader of Russia for over thirty years.

Why did Ulyanov shorten his name?

What meetings did Ulyanov attend?

Who was Lenin's friend?

How did they support their revolution against the Tsars?

Why is Karl Marx and Friedrich Engels important in history?

What idea did Lenin and Stalin sell the Russian people?

How did Lenin gain control of the people?

What did Lenin and Stalin call their gang?

How long did Lenin stay in power before leaving to live in Switzerland?

Francis Scott Key

President Madison declared war in 1812 on Great Britain because they captured our ships and men that traded with France. Dolly Madison saved important papers from the destruction of the British troops. British commanders defended the burning of the White House, the Supreme court in Washington, D.C. British sought revenge for the British Canadian capitol building in Toronto, Canada when it was destroyed in 1813 by Americans.

On another battle front, the British were hanging tough and a battle took place on Lake Erie. Commodore Oliver H. Perry had smaller ships than the British.

A young American Captain Macdonough was head of a fleet of small American ships on Lake Champlain. He was in the harbor of Plattsburg, and he met the larger British ships that had better equipment and outnumbered the American ships. Macdonough strategy was as brilliant as Perry's. The battle took place on September 11, a year after Commodore Perry's defeat of the British forces. The British navy retreated to Canada.

Americans by land would fight another large battle in New Orleans that would bring a close to the war that began in1812, with the United Kingdom. General Andrew Jackson taught his men to fight fiercely like the Indians. He and his men defeated the British Military.

In the meantime, an American fort was about to be attacked by the British navy. Key set foot on a British ship to negotiate the freedom of his doctor friend, Doctor William Beane. Therefore, Key was not allowed to leave the ship. He was held captive in September 1813 until 1814. He was held captive on the ship because he saw the battle plans of the British. When Francis awakened the next morning, he caught sight of the U.S. flag flying over Fort McHenry in Baltimore, Maryland. He quickly paid tribute to the American flag flying over Fort McHenry. The fort had survived the British attack.

In the early morning hours, he wrote the national anthem, "The Star Spangled Banner." The goal of the British was to separate and divide up the New England states from the vibrant and enthusiastic Mid-West and Southern states in America. After the war was won by Americans, Key became a successful lawyer in Maryland and in the Washington, D.C. area.

In the 1930's music was composed to fit the words of the Star Spangled Banner. President Wilson made the "Star Spangled Banner" America's National Anthem. Our flag is a precious sight to see because it represents freedom around the world.

What career did Francis Scott Key attain?

Why did Key leave his ship and board the British ship?

What did Francis Scott Key notice on board the British ship?

What happened to Key?

Why was Commodore Oliver H. Perry's battle important?

What did Perry do?

What year did the British try to capture New Orleans?

Heart

Did you know that muscles are in your stomach and intestine too? Muscles move the food in your body whether you are asleep or awake. A heart is a muscle that beats blood and keeps blood moving throughout the heart and into the valves within your heart and body.

The heart is divided into two chambers. The right side of the heart takes the rich oxygen blood and pumps it throughout the body. There are two upper chambers to the heart called the atria that receives blood as it returns to the heart. It has thin-walled chambers.

Blood arrives from other parts of the body and fills the right ventricle. In the right ventricle, the blood is then sent to the lungs and other tissues of the body. The walls of the ventricles are much thicker and muscular because it sends blood around the entire body. Each of the four valves have a flap on top to keep the blood flowing in the same direction. Electrical impulses are sent and keeps the beat of the heart moving. It becomes like a pacemaker for the heart.

The heart has two lower chambers below and they are called ventricles. They have muscular walls because of the force to send off blood to lungs and other tissues or parts of the body.

Did you know the heart has fourteen different valve openings in the body? Each valve receives or sends blood in or out of the body.

You can feel the heart beating by taking two fingers and placing on the neck, arm, under the knee or at the ankle. The heart moves voluntarily without your permission. It consistently beats night and day working in the body pumping blood. It never seems to tire out. It can pump 2,000 gallons of blood each day.

The average pulse is seventy times a minute. With physical exercise the body pulse rate becomes higher. Arteries and veins send and receive blood from the heart. Arteries and veins can be seen through the heart. They carry blood to the heart and away from the heart to nourish cells within the body.

What does the right ventricle do?

The right side of the heart is responsible for?

How many chambers to a heart?

What is the function of the left side of the heart?

Why do valves have flaps on top?

How many flaps does the heart have?

Clara Barton

Clara Barton was not a licensed nurse, and her first patient was her brother. He has fallen off the barn roof. Clara read and entertained her brother.

In the meantime, she listened to her father tell stories about the Revolutionary War, and how the soldiers had a rough time. Her father's stories made an impressive impression on Clara.

Clara decided she wanted to help people, and so she became a teacher to help students. At age sixteen, Clara started her own school and Was successful. Her first school was in New Jersey for students.

She decided to visit friends in Washington, D.C. Consequently, in

1865, a Civil War broke out. Some of the men from her town joined the Army and were wounded. She and other women in Washington, D.C. attended to the needs of the soldiers. They took medicine, bandages, food, and candles to help the soldiers.

Clara's father became ill, and she returned home to Massachusetts. Her father told more war stories and encouraged his daughter, Clara to follow her passion of nursing. Clara returned to Washington, D.C. and went straight to the battlefield to nurse soldiers back to health.

A surgeon named Clara the "Angel of the Battlefield" because she brought needed supplies for bandaging wounds. Clara never received professional nurse training, but she learned by her own experiences. She was self-taught and passed her knowledge on to others who would become nurses. Clara was anti-slavery but attended to the needs of wounded Confederate soldiers too.

Clara worked with the Union for four years tirelessly for the soldiers. After the war, Clara took a vacation in Switzerland. In Switzerland, she learned about twenty countries who started an organization to help people in tragedy. It was named the Red Cross.

Clara Barton became the first president of the Red Cross in America. She served for twenty-two years. If a tragedy occurred because of the storm, the Red Cross helped clothe people who lost everything.

An Englishman named Edward Howe convinced Clara to teach a First aid class. Clara got an apartment in New York and paid out of pocket for dolls to be used as models. The class was a success. Clara worked tirelessly writing books with her friends in Maryland about the Red Cross.

Who was Clara Barton?

Who was Clara's first patient?

Where did Clara live with her family?

How did the men on the battlefield feel about Clara?

What career did Clara choose?

How did she become involved with the Red Cross?

When did the Civil War take place?

What were Clara Barton's thoughts, feelings, ideas, and beliefs about the war?

James Madison

My name is James Madison and people ask me what contribution did I make for the American people? Well, I am one of the Founding Fathers who promoted the Bill of Rights in the Constitution that protects our freedom. The members of the Continental Congress were persuaded by me to accept the Constitution. I also co-authored the Federalist Papers with my friends, John Jay and Alexander Hamilton. The Federalist Papers helped to establish a system of checks and balances for the Federal government.

My presidency began in 1809. We traded goods with Britain and France. A year later, France and Britain were at war with one another. Britain refused to allow us to trade with France. Britain captured our cargo ships.

By 1812, my presidency was not a pleasant time because Great Britain was blockading American ships trading with France. So, Congress and I declared war on Britain in the month of June in the year 1812. It was the second time we were at war with Britain. British soldiers' set fire to The White House. They torched rooms in the Capitol, The Library of Congress, House of Representatives, Senate and Supreme Court.

On Christmas Eve on December 24, 1814, Britain surrendered by agreeing to the terms in the Treaty of Ghent that was signed in the Netherlands. However, the treaty did not take effect until February 1815. Peace came.

Progress was being made on a wide range of issues. We began construction on roads, and we reorganized the National Bank.

Who was James Madison?
What did Madison promote in the Constitution?
When did Madison become president?
What happened after a year of Madison presidency?
Why did Madison and Congress declare war on Britain?
What did the British do in the War of 1812?
When did Britain surrender?
What was the name of the treaty Britain and America signed?
When did the treaty take effect?

James Monroe

In 1817, James Monroe became the fifth president. A year into Monroe's presidency, a Convention was held in 1818, and the boundary between the Britain and the United States was agreed upon and became permanent.

In 1819, President James Monroe acquired Florida from Spain. Spain was a war and Great Britain. Spain needed money for the war against England. America negotiated and traded with Spain concerning commerce. Spain was in debt and agreed to sell Florida if the United States cancelled The debt of five million dollars. So, Florida was purchased from Spain.

The Westward movement in America created problems for Monroe when it came to having a slave state or a non-slave state. Spain and Great Britian were at war with each other. A dispute was about to take place but was halted temporarily. So, in 1820, The Missouri Compromise briefly halted the expansion of slavery into unsettled territory.
Both Northern Republicans and Democrats refused to include the territory of the Louisiana Purchase. They did not want to have a slave state. The Louisiana Purchase encompassed many states that would later ask for statehood. By 1823, Europeans were looking to expand their quest for additional territory in the Western Hemisphere. Monroe believed in nationalism for America.

Who become the fifth president?
What important decision became permanent in 1818?
What did President Monroe purchase from Europe in 1819?
What country did the U.S. trade within commerce?
What happened to Spain flourishing economy?

What did President Monroe cancel concerning Spain?

When did the Missouri Compromise happen?

What was the Missouri Compromise about?

What did Republicans and Democrats refuse to do?

While in high school prepare for a literature exam. A few classics are mentioned in the following list. The classic list may be on high school exit exams, college entrance and college exit exams.

- Nineteen Eighty-Four by George Orwell
- Candid by Voltaire
- Great Expectations by Charles Dickens
- Tom Jones and David Copperfield by Henry Fielding
- Gulliver's Travels by Johnathan Swift
- The Scarlet Letter by Nathaniel Hawthorne
- The Rime of the Ancient Mariner by Samuel Taylor Coleridge
- Carmen by George Bizet
- Jane Eyre and Withering Heights by Charlotte Bronte
- Frankenstein by Mary Shelly
- The Red and the Black by Charlotte Bronte
- The Last of the Mohicans by James Fenimore Cooper
- The Three Mustketeers' by Alexander Duma
- Vanity Fair by William Makepeace Thackery
- The Tragedy of Faust by Johann Wolfgang von Goethe

- The Lady of the Lake by Sir Walter Scott
- Ivanhoe by Sir Walter Scott
- Pride and Prejudice by Jane Austen
- Moby Dick by Herman Melville
- Silas Marner and Middlemarch by George Eliot
- Madam Bovary by Gustave Flaubert
- Idyls of the King by Alfred Lord Tennyson
- Little Women by Louisa May Alcott
- Far farm Madding Crowd by Thomas Hardy
- Crime and Punishment by Feodor Dostoyevsky
- The Brothers Karamazov by Feodor Dostoyevsky
- The Connecticut Yankee in King Arthur's Court by Mark Twain
- The Adventures of Huckleberry Finn by Mark Twain
- Anna Karenina by Leo Tolstoy
- The Devine Comedy by Dante Alighieri
- Hamlet by Shakespeare
- War and Peace and the Iliad by Leo Tolstoy
- The Odyssey by Homer

Conclusion

Over the years, I observed students who were struggling in reading did not like to read aloud in class in front of their peers. The older students know the names of the letters in the alphabet. Consonants, blends, and digraphs do not change in sound. It is the vowels that have different sounds. A young student and an older student will see the letter "a" but will not be able to hear or distinguish the sound. Therefore, an exaggeration of the letter "a" or any vowel should be exaggerated for a student to hear the difference. The student should imitate the sound so they can hear which pronunciation is correct.

Scores will increase when the literary terms have been taught to them by using index cards. By placing the word and the definition on the opposite side, a student can study the literary terms.

Comprehension is a learned skill. By reading and predicting what the title of the article is about, plays an important part training the brain to stay focused on reading. Also, taking time to predict each paragraph before reading it is crucial in reading and finding the correct answer to a prediction. Along the way, a student will learn to make judgements and will be capable of analyzing the outcome of an article.

Bibliography

Campodonica, Carol. <u>Rocket Reader 2</u>. Rocket Reading International. 2022

Encyclopedia Americana Corporation 1957 Edition.

http://www.freedictionary 2018

http://www.morewords 2018

http://www.spellzone.com 2018

http: //www.wordgmehlper.com 2018

http://www.Wordfinder/wordendings 2018

Ph.D, Jacqueline E. Kress Ed.D., Dona Lee Fountoukidis, Ed. D <u>The Reading Teachers Book of Lists by Edward Bernard Fry</u> Apprentice-Hall Inc., 1993.

<u>The Only Grammar Book You'll Ever Need</u> by Susan Thurman Adams Media, Avon Massachusetts 2023

www.ingramcontent.com/pod-product-compliance
Lightning Source LLC
Chambersburg PA
CBHW061807290426
44109CB00031B/2956